The Demise of Higher Education

How Colleges and Universities Betray Students for Profit

Douglas B Sims, PhD

DB Sims, PhD

Book design by DB Sims
Cover design by DB Sims

ISBN – Paperback: 978-1-966739-01-2
ISBN – eBook: 978-1-966739-00-5

First Edition: February 2025

Table of Contents

Acknowledgements

I am deeply grateful to my wife, whose unwavering support, wisdom, and love have been the cornerstone of our incredible 34-year journey together. You have been both my anchor and my inspiration, enriching every step of our shared path and guiding me through life's twists and turns.

To our two children, thank you for the immense joy, growth, and life lessons you have brought into our world. Watching you grow and embrace life has been one of the greatest privileges of my life, filling it with pride, discovery, and endless gratitude.

I also wish to extend heartfelt thanks to my friends and colleagues. Your insights, shared experiences, and willingness to engage in meaningful conversations have profoundly shaped this book. The authenticity and depth you've added through your stories and perspectives have been truly invaluable. I am sincerely grateful for the openness and contributions that have enriched this journey and this work.

Forward

The American Dream—a promise of opportunity, upward mobility, and a better life—has always been intertwined with the transformative power of education. For generations, colleges and universities served as gateways to this dream, opening doors to careers, financial security, and societal progress. Yet today, higher education in America stands at a crossroads. Skyrocketing tuition, overwhelming student debt, and a growing disconnect between academic programs and workforce needs have undermined its promise. For many, the dream of education as the ultimate equalizer feels more like an unattainable illusion.

This book tackles the critical question: How did we get here, and what must be done to reclaim the potential of higher education?

Through a sharp examination of systemic flaws, this book explores how colleges and universities have strayed from their purpose, prioritizing prestige and profit over accessibility and equity. Rising costs have locked out countless students, leaving them burdened with debt or unable to attend. Curricula often fail to meet the demands of a rapidly evolving economy, leaving graduates unprepared. The problem is compounded by the proliferation of degrees that offer little value in the job market. Fields like sociology and philosophy, while intellectually enriching, often fail to translate into career-ready skills, leaving graduates burdened by debt and struggling to find meaningful employment. These programs highlight a troubling disconnect between higher education and workforce demands.

Moreover, the inefficiencies in professional degree pathways, such as those for medical doctors (MDs), dentists (DDS/DMDs), and others, further underscore the need for reform. In the United States, these degrees often take three to four years longer than necessary due to outdated requirements, such as completing a bachelor's degree before beginning medical or dental school. In contrast, countries like the United Kingdom and Australia streamline these pathways, allowing students to enter directly into professional programs after high school, saving time and reducing financial strain. These extended timelines in the U.S. not only contribute to the mounting cost of education but also delay the entry of qualified professionals into critical fields.

Yet, higher education remains one of the most powerful tools we have to build a fairer, more prosperous society—if we are willing to confront its failings. This book is both a critique and a call to action. It doesn't simply diagnose the problems but envisions a future where colleges and universities are reinvigorated as engines of opportunity, innovation, and social change. It challenges us to make higher education affordable, accessible, and aligned with the demands of the 21st century. From rethinking tuition models to fostering industry partnerships, from embedding civic responsibility into academic programs to investing in student success, the path forward is clear, but it requires bold action and collective will.

This is a book for anyone who believes in the power of education to shape lives and societies. Whether you are a student navigating the challenges of college, a parent questioning the return on investment, an educator grappling with inequities, or a policymaker tasked with shaping the future, this work will inspire you to imagine what is possible.

The American Dream is not dead—it is waiting to be reclaimed. Through innovation, commitment, and a shared belief in the transformative power of education, we can restore higher education's promise as the cornerstone of opportunity and progress for all. This book offers an essential guide to reviving that vision and ensuring the dream endures for generations to come.

Chapter 1

The Founding Mission: Education for a Better Society

Education has always been the bedrock of progress, a powerful force capable of shaping not only individuals but entire societies. The founding mission of American colleges and universities was driven by an ambitious ideal: to cultivate informed leaders, ethical citizens, and critical thinkers who could elevate the nation toward a better future. From the austere halls of colonial colleges preparing ministers and civic leaders to the sprawling campuses opened to millions through transformative policies like the GI Bill, higher education has mirrored the aspirations and struggles of American society. This chapter delves into the origins of this enduring mission, the rise of the liberal arts ideal as a beacon for intellectual freedom, and the revolutionary post-World War II expansion that redefined who could access the promise of a college education. These pivotal moments reveal a compelling narrative of resilience, reinvention, and the unyielding belief that education holds the key to a more equitable and enlightened world.

The Origins of American Colleges and Universities

The origins of American higher education are deeply rooted in the European tradition, specifically in the educational systems of England. The establishment of Harvard College in 1636, widely regarded as the first institution of higher learning in the United States, set the tone for American education. Its mission was closely tied to training clergy and leaders who would uphold religious and civic values in the New World. Harvard's motto, *Veritas* (Truth), reflected its focus on moral and intellectual development within a Puritan framework (Rudolph, 1990).

During the colonial period, colleges like Yale (1701), Princeton (1746), and the College of William and Mary (1693) were established with similar objectives. These institutions emphasized classical education, rooted in subjects like theology, Latin, and philosophy. Education was seen as a means to prepare a small, elite segment of society for leadership roles, both in the church and in governance. Access to education was highly limited, and students were predominantly white males from affluent backgrounds.

The 19th century brought significant changes with the passage of the Morrill Land-Grant Acts in 1862 and 1890. These acts provided federal land to states to fund public universities, fundamentally reshaping American higher education. The new land-grant institutions, such as Michigan State University and Iowa State University, expanded the curriculum beyond classical studies to include agriculture, mechanical arts, and engineering. This shift was a response to the industrialization and urbanization of America, emphasizing the practical application of education to address societal and economic needs (Thelin, 2011).

By the late 19th and early 20th centuries, universities began adopting the German research university model, emphasizing specialized fields of study, academic freedom, and the pursuit of knowledge for its own sake. This blending of classical education with practical and research-focused approaches created the uniquely American system of higher education that exists today.

The Liberal Arts Ideal: Cultivating Well-Rounded, Critical Thinkers

The liberal arts ideal has been a defining feature of American higher education since its inception. The term "liberal arts" originates from the Latin *artes liberales*, which referred to the skills necessary for a free person to actively participate in civic life during ancient Greece and Rome. These included grammar, rhetoric, logic, arithmetic, geometry, music, and astronomy. The goal was to cultivate an individual who was knowledgeable, articulate, and capable of critical thought (Kimball, 1995).

In the early American colleges, liberal arts curricula emphasized classical studies such as Greek, Latin, and philosophy, alongside theology. This approach reflected the belief that education should develop moral character and intellectual rigor. Students were expected to become well-rounded individuals who could contribute meaningfully to society, whether as clergy, civic leaders, or scholars.

The industrial revolution and the rise of specialized fields in the 19th and 20th centuries challenged the liberal arts ideal. As vocational and professional education gained prominence, critics questioned the practicality of a broad-based education. Yet, proponents of the liberal arts argued that this approach remained essential for developing critical thinking, adaptability, and a sense of ethical responsibility—qualities vital in an increasingly complex world (Delbanco, 2012).

In contemporary times, liberal arts education continues to face scrutiny as students and parents prioritize degrees that lead directly to employment. However, many colleges and universities maintain that the liberal arts foster skills such as communication, creativity, and problem-solving, which are highly valued by employers across industries. Institutions have adapted by integrating liberal arts principles into interdisciplinary and applied learning frameworks, ensuring that the ideal remains relevant in a rapidly changing world.

Post-WWII Transformation: The GI Bill and Expanding Access to Higher Education

The end of World War II ushered in a new era for higher education in the United States. The Servicemen's Readjustment Act of 1944, better known as the GI Bill, represented one of the most transformative policies in the history of American education. It provided returning veterans with unprecedented access to higher education by covering tuition costs, offering living allowances, and providing financial support for books and supplies (Bound & Turner, 2002).

The impact of the GI Bill was immediate and profound. Over 2 million veterans took advantage of the educational benefits between 1945 and 1956, dramatically increasing college enrollments and fundamentally altering the demographic composition of the student population. For the first time, higher education became accessible to individuals from working-class and rural backgrounds who had previously been excluded from such opportunities.

This democratization of education also led to significant institutional changes. Colleges and universities expanded their campuses, built new facilities, and developed programs to accommodate the surge in enrollment. The increased diversity among students brought new perspectives and challenges to academia, prompting institutions to rethink their curricula and support systems (Hutcheson, 2007).

The GI Bill's legacy extends beyond individual educational attainment. It contributed to the rise of a robust middle class in post-war America, fostering economic growth and social mobility. Moreover, it established the principle that higher education is a public good, deserving of federal investment to benefit society at large. However, it also exposed inequities, as many Black veterans faced discrimination and were often denied access to the benefits in the segregated South (Mettler, 2005).

The post-WWII era solidified higher education's role as a cornerstone of American society. The expansion of access and the growing diversity of the student body set the stage for further developments in the latter half of the 20th century, including the Civil Rights Movement, the women's rights movement, and the continued evolution of higher education policy.

The story of American higher education is one of vision, resilience, and transformation. From its modest beginnings in colonial colleges to its post-war expansion into a powerful engine of social mobility, higher education has consistently evolved to meet the changing needs of society. The enduring commitment to cultivating informed, critical thinkers through the liberal arts, paired with efforts to expand access through groundbreaking initiatives like the GI Bill, reflects a deep belief in education as a tool for individual empowerment and societal progress. However, over time, higher education has begun to falter, constrained by a fear of change and a growing entanglement with industry that prioritizes immediate profits over long-term learning and innovation. As a result, institutions are increasingly failing to adequately prepare students for the complexities of modern life and the evolving needs of industry. While the foundational mission remains clear—to use education as a force for building a more just and thriving society—its realization now demands a renewed willingness to adapt and engage. As we look to the future, this legacy of adaptation and innovation serves not only as a reminder of what is possible but as an urgent call to action to reclaim education's transformative potential.

Chapter 2

The Growth of Public Colleges and Universities

The growth of public colleges and universities represents one of the most transformative developments in American education, redefining access and opportunity for millions. These institutions, from the establishment of land-grant universities in the 19th century to the rise of community colleges in the 20th, have been pivotal in democratizing education and meeting the needs of an evolving society. By prioritizing affordability and aligning education with workforce demands, public higher education has become a cornerstone of economic growth, social mobility, and community development. This chapter explores how public colleges and universities have not only expanded the reach of higher education but also shaped the nation's future by providing a pathway to success for individuals from all walks of life.

The Rise of Community Colleges and State Universities

The emergence of community colleges and state universities marked a significant shift in American higher education, emphasizing accessibility, practicality, and local engagement. Community colleges, initially termed "junior colleges," were conceived in the early 20th century to address the educational needs of a rapidly industrializing society. Institutions like Joliet Junior College, founded in 1901, served as pioneers of a new model of education that provided the first two years of undergraduate study and vocational training. By the 1920s, community colleges had gained traction, with leaders like William Rainey Harper championing their role in bridging the gap between secondary and higher education (Cohen et al., 2014).

State universities have an even earlier genesis, rooted in the Morrill Land-Grant Acts of 1862 and 1890. These landmark pieces of legislation provided federal lands to states to establish public universities that emphasized agriculture, mechanical arts, and engineering. This approach democratized higher education by expanding its reach beyond the elite classical colleges, making it accessible to the working class. Institutions like the University of Wisconsin and Michigan State University exemplified this land-grant model, fostering innovation and economic growth through research and practical education (Thelin, 2011).

The post-World War II era brought unprecedented growth for public higher education. The GI Bill enabled millions of veterans to attend college, creating a demand for new campuses and programs. This period saw the establishment of community colleges nationwide, as states recognized the need for localized, low-cost institutions to accommodate diverse populations. By the mid-20th century, public colleges and universities had become integral to the fabric of American society, providing education that was not only accessible but also responsive to the economic and social needs of the time.

The Promise of Affordable Education for Local Communities

Affordability has been a cornerstone of public colleges and universities, particularly community colleges, which were designed to provide low-cost education to local residents. This mission was founded on the belief that proximity and affordability were critical to democratizing access to education. Community colleges were structured with open admissions policies, minimal tuition fees, and flexible schedules to accommodate nontraditional students, including working adults, veterans, and recent high school graduates (Bailey et al., 2015).

State universities have also historically offered affordable education. The financial model of state-supported higher education relied on taxpayer funding to subsidize tuition, ensuring that residents could access quality education at a fraction of the cost of private institutions. For much of the 20th century, this model worked effectively, enabling a generation of Americans to attend college without incurring significant debt. The economic benefits of this approach were clear: affordable public education allowed students from diverse socioeconomic backgrounds to enter higher education and improve their career prospects (Huelsman, 2018).

However, the affordability promise has faced increasing challenges. Since the 1980s, declining state funding for higher education has shifted the financial burden onto students, resulting in rising tuition costs. Community colleges, while still relatively low-cost, often struggle with limited resources, which can impact the quality of education and student support services. State universities, once affordable for most families, now see many students relying heavily on loans to finance their education. This shift has led to a growing student debt crisis, raising questions about the long-term sustainability of public higher education's affordability mission (Thelin, 2011).

Despite these challenges, public colleges and universities continue to innovate to maintain affordability. Dual-enrollment programs, partnerships with local high schools, and targeted financial aid initiatives have helped mitigate costs for many students. For example, the Tennessee Promise program offers free community college tuition for eligible high school graduates, serving as a model for states seeking to fulfill the affordability mission of public higher education (Bailey et al., 2015).

The Role of Colleges in Workforce Development and Social Mobility

Public colleges and universities are indispensable to workforce development, aligning their programs with the needs of local and national economies. Community colleges, in particular, have been leaders in offering career-focused education. Programs in fields such as healthcare, information technology, and skilled trades prepare students for immediate employment, meeting the demand for middle-skill jobs that require more than a high school diploma but less than a bachelor's degree. For example, many community colleges partner with local industries to create customized training programs, ensuring that graduates have the skills employers need (Carnevale et al., 2012).

State universities play a complementary role by offering advanced degrees in critical fields, such as engineering, education, and business. Many state universities work directly with industry leaders to ensure that their curricula align with workforce demands. Cooperative education programs, internships, and research collaborations allow students to gain hands-on experience while contributing to industry innovation. Institutions like Purdue University and the University of Michigan are known for their strong ties to industries, driving regional economic development while preparing graduates for high-demand careers (Levin et al., 2010).

Beyond workforce development, public colleges and universities are engines of social mobility. Research shows that higher education is one of the most effective pathways for individuals to improve their economic standing. Graduates of public colleges earn significantly more over their lifetimes than those with only a high school diploma, creating opportunities for upward mobility that extend to their families and communities (Chetty et al., 2017).

Moreover, public institutions have been instrumental in addressing educational inequities. Community colleges often serve as entry points for underrepresented populations, including students of color, first-generation college students, and immigrants. By offering affordable, accessible education, these institutions provide pathways to higher degrees and career advancement. Similarly, state universities have expanded efforts to support diverse student populations through scholarships, mentorship programs, and targeted retention initiatives.

Despite these successes, challenges remain. Graduation rates at community colleges and state universities vary widely, and many students face barriers such as financial instability, lack of academic preparation, and limited access to support services. Addressing these challenges will be critical to ensuring that public colleges and universities continue to fulfill their role in promoting workforce development and social mobility.

The expansion of public colleges and universities has profoundly shaped the landscape of American higher education, opening doors to millions and driving societal progress. These institutions have fulfilled vital roles, from offering affordable education to fostering workforce development and advancing social mobility. Yet, as they continue to adapt to evolving challenges, including rising costs and shifting workforce demands, their mission remains as critical as ever. The promise of public higher education lies in its ability to empower individuals, strengthen communities, and drive economic and social innovation. To sustain this promise, it is essential to reinvest in the accessibility, affordability, and quality of these institutions, ensuring that they remain beacons of opportunity for generations to come. In a rapidly changing world, the enduring mission of public colleges and universities to serve the greater good stands as a testament to their indispensable role in building a stronger, more equitable society.

Chapter 3

Skyrocketing Costs and the Student Debt Crisis

The skyrocketing costs of higher education in the United States have transformed the promise of opportunity into a burden of debt for millions of students. What was once seen as a pathway to social mobility and economic security is now often accompanied by financial strain that shapes life choices and limits opportunities. Tuition rates have risen exponentially over the past several decades, driven by declining public funding, increasing administrative costs, and the expansion of student loan systems. While colleges and universities benefit from this debt-driven model, students and graduates face the long-term consequences of borrowing, from restricted career options to delayed milestones like homeownership and family formation. This chapter examines the forces behind the explosion of tuition costs, the role of the student loan industry in perpetuating the crisis, and the far-reaching economic and social impacts of student debt on individuals and society.

Explaining the Explosion of Tuition Costs

The relentless increase in college tuition costs has become a defining feature of higher education in the United States, placing immense financial pressure on students and families. Over the past four decades, tuition at public four-year universities has risen by more than 213%, while private nonprofit institutions have experienced increases of 144% (Baum & Ma, 2020). This staggering growth is the result of a complex interplay of economic, political, and institutional factors that have reshaped the financial landscape of higher education.

One of the most significant contributors to rising tuition is the decline in state funding for public colleges and universities. Historically, state governments played a central role in subsidizing higher education, ensuring that tuition remained affordable for residents. However, economic downturns, particularly the 2008 financial crisis, prompted severe budget cuts in many states, leading to a shift in costs from taxpayers to students. Between 2008 and 2018, average state funding per student dropped by 13%, with some states cutting funding by as much as 40% (Mitchell et al., 2019). This decrease forced public institutions to increase tuition to cover operating expenses, eroding the affordability that once defined public higher education.

Another factor driving tuition increases is the growing administrative costs at colleges and universities. Institutions have significantly expanded their non-academic staff to meet the demands of modern student services, regulatory compliance, and competitive marketing efforts. While these expansions address important needs such as mental health services and career counseling, they also contribute to higher operational costs. Critics argue that this administrative bloat, coupled with investments in luxury amenities like state-of-the-art dormitories, buildings, and recreational facilities, has diverted resources from academic programs and increased tuition unnecessarily (Vedder, 2021).

Inflation in faculty compensation has been less of a driver than often assumed, as many institutions have shifted toward employing adjunct and part-time faculty at lower salaries. Despite these cost-saving measures, tuition has continued to climb, as the savings are often reallocated to other areas of institutional spending (Kezar et al., 2019). Rising healthcare and pension costs for faculty and staff have also added financial strain, further pushing tuition upward.

Finally, the growing reliance on federal financial aid, including loans and grants, has unintentionally contributed to tuition hikes. Known as the "Bennett hypothesis," this theory posits that as federal aid availability increases, colleges raise tuition to capture more of the financial aid dollars. While this relationship remains debated, the accessibility of federal loans has undoubtedly enabled institutions to increase costs without fear of pricing students out of attendance (Baum, 2016).

The Student Loan Industry: How Colleges Benefit from Indebted Students

The student loan industry has transformed from a tool for improving educational access into a massive economic enterprise that benefits colleges, lenders, and financial institutions while leaving students saddled with debt. Federal loans, initially introduced in the 1950s to support low-income students, have expanded significantly over time. Today, student loans are the primary mechanism through which many Americans finance their education, creating a system where the financial risks of higher education disproportionately fall on the borrowers rather than the institutions (Collinge, 2009).

One of the critical issues with the current system is the interplay between rising tuition costs and the federal financial aid model. Federal student loans are often awarded based on tuition costs, which incentivizes colleges to raise tuition, knowing that increased financial aid will cover the gap. This borrower-based funding model has created a feedback loop: as tuition rises, loan limits increase, allowing students to borrow more. Colleges, in turn, benefit from a steady revenue stream with little incentive to contain costs, as federal loans are guaranteed regardless of whether students succeed academically or financially (Baum, 2016).

Private student loans further exacerbate the problem. While federal loans come with relatively low-interest rates and flexible repayment options, private loans often have higher interest rates and fewer consumer protections. Many colleges partner with private lenders, encouraging students to take out loans to cover the gap between federal aid and tuition costs. These arrangements often prioritize institutional revenue over student well-being, leading to higher debt burdens for borrowers (Looney & Yannelis, 2019).

For-profit colleges have been particularly criticized for their role in exploiting the student loan system. These institutions often target low-income and nontraditional students, promising lucrative career outcomes while delivering subpar educational experiences. For-profit colleges receive a significant portion of their revenue from federal financial aid programs, yet their students are more likely to default on loans and experience poor employment outcomes (Cellini & Turner, 2019). Despite regulatory efforts to curb these practices, the financialization of higher education continues to disproportionately harm the most vulnerable students.

Colleges and universities benefit not only from the influx of tuition dollars but also from the broader economic ecosystem surrounding student loans. Alumni donations, endowments, and federal research grants often depend on the perception of institutional success, which rising enrollments and higher tuition can bolster. However, this revenue-driven approach has left many graduates struggling to manage debt, undermining the very mission of higher education as a pathway to opportunity and mobility.

The Financial Burden on Graduates and Its Long-Term Effects on the Economy

The financial burden of student loan debt has reached crisis levels in the United States, with over 44 million borrowers collectively owing more than $1.8 trillion as of 2023 (Federal Reserve Bank of New York, 2023). For individual graduates, the average debt at graduation is approximately $37,000, but for many, particularly those who pursue advanced degrees or attend private institutions, this number is significantly higher. The weight of this debt extends far beyond financial strain, shaping life choices and limiting economic opportunities.

One of the most immediate impacts of student debt is its influence on career decisions. Graduates with high levels of debt often feel compelled to prioritize high-paying jobs over positions in public service or creative fields. This trend not only restricts personal fulfillment but also deprives sectors like education, healthcare, and the arts of much-needed talent (Ambrose et al., 2021).

Homeownership, a traditional marker of economic stability, is also negatively impacted by student debt. Borrowers often delay purchasing homes due to limited savings and lower credit scores, contributing to a decline in homeownership rates among young adults. Research shows that for every $1,000 increase in student loan debt, homeownership rates drop by approximately 1.5% (Mezza et al., 2020). This delay has broader economic implications, as reduced homeownership affects industries ranging from construction to retail.

The student debt crisis also hinders wealth accumulation and exacerbates generational and racial wealth gaps. Black and Hispanic borrowers, who are more likely to rely on loans to finance their education, face higher default rates and greater difficulty repaying their loans. This disparity limits their ability to invest in assets, save for retirement, or build intergenerational wealth, perpetuating systemic inequality (Addo et al., 2016).

At a macroeconomic level, the student debt crisis reduces consumer spending and economic growth. Borrowers allocate significant portions of their income to loan repayment, limiting discretionary spending on goods, services, and investments. High debt levels also discourage entrepreneurship, as potential business owners face difficulty securing credit or taking financial risks while managing existing obligations (Ambrose et al., 2021).

The psychological toll of student debt is equally significant. Borrowers frequently report high levels of stress, anxiety, and depression related to their financial obligations. These mental health challenges can affect productivity, job performance, and overall quality of life. For those who default on their loans, the consequences are even more severe, including wage garnishment, damaged credit, and legal repercussions (Walsemann et al., 2015).

Addressing the student debt crisis requires systemic reform, including policy changes to make higher education more affordable and accessible. Proposals such as expanding income-driven repayment plans, increasing federal investment in public colleges, and implementing targeted debt forgiveness programs aim to alleviate the burden on borrowers while encouraging institutions to control costs. These solutions, however, must be accompanied by a cultural shift that values education as a public good rather than a private commodity, ensuring that future generations can pursue higher learning without fear of financial ruin.

The student debt crisis stands as one of the most pressing challenges in American higher education, underscoring deep systemic flaws in how we fund and value learning. The unchecked rise in tuition costs, coupled with a profit-driven student loan industry, has left millions of graduates saddled with debt that constrains their personal and professional lives. This burden extends beyond individuals, weakening economic growth, perpetuating inequality, and limiting opportunities for future generations. While education remains a critical pathway to personal and societal advancement, its growing inaccessibility threatens its transformative potential. To address this crisis, we must reimagine higher education funding—prioritizing affordability, accountability, and equity—while advocating for systemic reforms that place students' futures above institutional profits. The solutions to this challenge lie not only in policy changes but also in a collective commitment to restoring education as a public good that empowers individuals and strengthens communities.

Chapter 4

The Myth of "The More It Costs, The Better It Is"

Universities often perpetuate the notion that higher tuition equals higher quality, creating a perception that elite institutions offering expensive programs provide a superior education. This marketing strategy plays on the fears of students and parents who view college as the golden ticket to a prosperous future. As a result, many students willingly take on massive loans, believing that a prestigious degree justifies the cost and will guarantee long-term financial success. However, the reality is often far more sobering.

Graduates frequently leave college burdened with debts that can exceed four times their first year's professional salary, particularly in fields like education, social work, or journalism, where entry-level pay is modest. According to data from the National Center for Education Statistics (NCES), the average debt for students earning a bachelor's degree is approximately $30,000, but many graduates in certain fields accumulate significantly more debt (NCES, 2022). For instance, in 2022, social workers reported a median starting salary of $42,000, while educators earned an average of $41,000 annually (Bureau of Labor Statistics [BLS], 2023). Meanwhile, journalists earned a median entry-level salary of $44,000, which, compared to debt burdens nearing or exceeding $100,000, places these graduates in a precarious financial position (BLS, 2023).

The financial strain of high student debt disproportionately affects individuals entering lower-paying professions. A graduate with $100,000 in student loans and a $40,000 starting salary could face monthly loan payments of $1,000 or more under a standard 10-year repayment plan, consuming 30% or more of their gross income (Federal Student Aid, 2023). This debt-to-income ratio exceeds recommended financial thresholds, such as the 20% guideline advocated by financial experts, which suggests student loan payments should not exceed 20% of discretionary income (Consumer Financial Protection Bureau [CFPB], 2021).

These financial burdens often delay critical life milestones. A study by the Federal Reserve found that student loan debt is one of the primary reasons millennials postpone homeownership, with 22% citing it as a major barrier (Federal Reserve, 2021). Additionally, research from the National Association of Realtors revealed that student debt contributes to delaying marriage, starting a family, and saving for retirement (National Association of Realtors [NAR], 2022). This delay in wealth-building activities exacerbates long-term financial insecurity, further entrenching socioeconomic inequalities.

Beyond personal finances, the societal impacts of excessive student debt are significant. As graduates channel a large portion of their income toward loan repayment, their ability to participate fully in the economy diminishes. Reduced consumer spending on housing, cars, and other major purchases has a ripple effect, slowing overall economic growth (Looney & Yannelis, 2022). This underscores the urgent need for systemic reforms to align education costs with career outcomes and to provide more equitable financial pathways for students pursuing lower-paying professions

What College Should Cost: Aligning Education Costs with Future Income

To make higher education financially sustainable, students and families need to consider the relationship between the cost of a degree and the income it is likely to generate. A practical rule of thumb is that total student debt should not exceed the anticipated first-year salary of the graduate's chosen profession. For instance, a nursing student expecting a $60,000 starting salary should aim to graduate with no more than $60,000 in total debt. This alignment ensures that loan repayments remain manageable and that the financial return on education justifies the investment.

However, this level of financial planning is often absent. Many students, encouraged by parents and counselors, assume that any level of debt is acceptable because a college degree is seen as a universal key to financial security. This misplaced faith in higher education leads to reckless borrowing, with little consideration for how it will impact long-term financial stability.

The Illusion of Guaranteed Payoff

The belief that "a college degree pays off no matter the cost" is deeply ingrained in American culture. Parents, who came of age in an era when a bachelor's degree nearly guaranteed a stable job and upward mobility, often encourage their children to prioritize prestigious and expensive institutions, viewing these as investments that will inevitably pay off. This mindset persists despite growing evidence that the return on investment (ROI) for higher education varies widely depending on the field of study and the cost of the degree. Research from the Georgetown University Center on Education and the Workforce indicates that while STEM, healthcare, and business degrees often provide strong lifetime earnings, many degrees in the arts, humanities, and social sciences offer significantly lower ROI (Carnevale et al., 2021).

Young adults are frequently bombarded with marketing messages from universities, emphasizing their alumni's success stories and implying that higher tuition correlates with higher quality education. These narratives obscure the reality that many graduates face significant challenges in today's labor market. For instance, a study by the Strada Education Network found that nearly 40% of college graduates work in jobs that do not require a degree, a phenomenon known as underemployment (Strada Education Network, 2022).

I recently spoke with a young woman who epitomizes the harsh financial realities of this system. She owed $250,000 in student loans for her bachelor's degree and was struggling to make ends meet. Despite her degree, she felt trapped in low-paying jobs and saw no viable path to financial stability. Her solution? Return to school to earn a JD degree in the hopes of securing a higher-paying job to pay off her existing student debt. This cycle of accumulating debt in pursuit of financial security is not uncommon.

The situation is equally bleak for some medical professionals. I know several individuals with MD degrees who, despite their extensive education, struggle to make a living. These doctors—general practitioners, pediatricians, and similar medical professionals—earn approximately $150,000 annually but often carry student loan debts of $250,000 or more. Their high debt-to-income ratio leaves them financially strained, with monthly loan payments rivaling or exceeding their living expenses.

But what about those who earn degrees in fields like modern literature, sociology, anthropology, or the history of science? Where are they supposed to work to earn a living that allows them to repay hefty student loans? Many of these graduates, despite their intellectual accomplishments, face grim job prospects. The reality for too many is a future of low-wage, unrelated employment. Will these graduates end up working at Walmart or in other service jobs, unable to utilize their education and trapped under the weight of their student debt?

Structural changes in the economy, including the rise of automation, outsourcing, and the gig economy, have further disrupted traditional career paths. According to McKinsey & Company, up to 25% of jobs in the U.S. are at risk of being displaced by automation by 2030, disproportionately affecting middle-skill occupations that historically provided stable employment for graduates (Manyika et al., 2017). These trends have left many graduates underemployed or working in fields unrelated to their degrees, further undermining the financial value of their education.

This growing disconnect between the cost of higher education and its economic benefits reveals a system that not only fails to deliver on its promises but actively misleads parents and students. Universities perpetuate the myth of guaranteed financial success to generate revenue and sustain their bloated administrative structures (Ginsberg, 2011). Parents and students must demand greater transparency and accountability, and the higher education system must prioritize affordability and ROI to ensure its long-term viability.

The Ripple Effects of Unsustainable Debt

The consequences of excessive student debt ripple far beyond the individual borrower. As graduates struggle to meet monthly payments, they often delay contributing to the economy, whether through purchasing homes, starting businesses, or investing in retirement accounts. According to the Federal Reserve, student loan debt is one of the primary reasons millennials and Gen Z delay homeownership, with 22% of borrowers citing it as a significant barrier (Federal Reserve, 2021). This economic stagnation not only affects individual financial health but also undermines broader economic growth, as reduced consumer spending impacts industries ranging from real estate to retail.

The psychological toll of student debt cannot be overlooked. Anxiety about looming debt leads to increased stress, mental health challenges, and reduced overall well-being. For many, the dream of higher education becomes a lifelong financial burden, contradicting its original promise of opportunity and upward mobility. A survey conducted by the American Psychological Association revealed that student loan debt is a leading cause of financial stress among young adults, often contributing to feelings of hopelessness and depression (APA, 2022).

On average, it takes borrowers about 20 years to fully repay their student loans, with some requiring 25 years or more, depending on the repayment plan and interest rates (U.S. Department of Education, 2023). This means that many individuals are still paying off their loans well into their 40s or even 50s, long after the supposed benefits of their degree should have materialized. For those in lower-paying fields or with significant debt balances, the repayment period can stretch even further, forcing graduates to delay or forgo other financial goals, such as saving for retirement or their children's education.

The average student loan debt for someone earning a bachelor's degree is approximately $30,000, but this number rises dramatically for those pursuing advanced degrees. Master's degree graduates accumulate an average of $66,000 in debt, while those earning a PhD take on an additional $108,000, bringing the total average debt for a student completing all three degrees to around $204,000 (NCES, 2022).

In contrast, my own educational experience paints a different picture. For my BA, MS, and PhD, I took out a total of $46,000 in student loans and managed to pay it off in under eight years. While that repayment timeline was achievable, it's important to note that my debt burden was significantly lower than what many students face today. Had my debt aligned with the current averages—closer to $204,000— my financial trajectory would likely have been far more difficult, and achieving financial stability within a decade might have been impossible.

This prolonged debt repayment perpetuates a cycle of financial insecurity, making it difficult for borrowers to build wealth or achieve long-term financial stability. The ripple effects extend to families and communities, with parents often taking on additional debt or cosigning loans, thereby jeopardizing their own financial futures. The broader societal impact underscores the urgent need for systemic reforms to address the affordability of higher education and the burden of student loan debt.

Rethinking the Value of a College Degree

To address these challenges, students and parents must adopt a more discerning approach to higher education. This begins with recognizing that a bachelor's degree is just that—a bachelor's degree. Its value lies in the accreditation of the institution and the knowledge gained, not in the prestige of the school's name, sports teams, or social scene. As long as the degree is from an accredited school, where you earn it matters far less than many assume. Choosing an institution based on weekend parties, luxury dorms, or athletic fame is a misguided approach that can saddle graduates with crippling debt for minimal additional benefit.

Students must also understand that going into more than $40,000 of debt for a bachelor's degree, as of 2025, is a sign of attending the wrong school. The goal should be to choose the right university—one that offers affordable, quality education—rather than the flashiest or most socially appealing option. Institutions such as community colleges, trade schools, and public universities often provide high-quality education at a fraction of the cost of elite private colleges, making them practical and financially sound choices. These schools offer pathways to the same careers without the burdensome financial strain of excessive student loans.

Moreover, universities must bear greater responsibility for the financial well-being of their students. Transparency in costs, honest communication about job prospects, and efforts to control tuition inflation are critical steps toward ensuring that higher education remains a path to opportunity rather than a trap of financial despair. Universities should also focus on providing resources that improve academic and career outcomes, such as robust advising programs, internship opportunities, and connections to local industries, rather than prioritizing costly, non-essential amenities.

In a world where the cost of education is often disconnected from its economic value, it is time to challenge the notion that more expensive always means better. By realigning educational investments with realistic career outcomes, students can avoid the pitfalls of unsustainable debt and achieve the financial security that higher education promises. Adopting this practical approach empowers students to take control of their financial futures, ensuring that their college experience leads to real opportunities rather than a lifetime of debt.

Chapter 5

Administrative Bloat and Misaligned Priorities

Administrative bloat and misaligned priorities have become defining challenges in modern higher education, reshaping the mission of colleges and universities. What were once institutions devoted to academic excellence and intellectual discovery now grapple with ballooning administrative costs and a growing emphasis on luxury amenities. The rise of non-academic administrators has diluted faculty influence, while investments in climbing walls, gourmet dining halls, buildings, and luxury dormitories overshadow the funding of classrooms and research. These trends not only burden students with higher tuition but also reflect a troubling shift in institutional values, where image and marketability often trump education and equity. This chapter examines the root causes of administrative expansion, the allure of non-essential amenities, and the devastating consequences of budget mismanagement, urging a reevaluation of priorities to restore higher education's foundational purpose.

Athletics Over Academics

A particularly glaring example of misaligned priorities is the disproportionate emphasis on collegiate athletics. The so-called "sports arms race" has driven universities to pour staggering amounts of money into building state-of-the-art stadiums, hiring high-profile coaches, and funding athletic programs in hopes of boosting enrollment, visibility, and alumni donations. This focus often comes at the expense of academic investment, with resources diverted from classrooms and research to maintain competitive sports programs.

For many students, the reputation of a university's sports teams significantly influences their choice of institution. Colleges capitalize on this trend by branding their campuses as centers of athletic prestige, allocating millions to build facilities that rival professional sports complexes. For instance, Clemson University's $55 million football operations complex, complete with a bowling alley and nap rooms, epitomizes the prioritization of athletics over academics. Similarly, the University of Alabama, with its $92 million Bryant-Denny Stadium renovation, and the University of Oregon, which boasts a $68 million football performance center funded largely by Nike co-founder Phil Knight, highlight the lavish investments funneled into athletics. Meanwhile, academic departments at these institutions face hiring freezes, larger class sizes, and outdated resources.

This is where it goes wrong for the education of today's American students: athletics are prioritized over state-of-the-art labs, modern classrooms, competitive faculty salaries, and the essential infrastructure needed for institutional operations. Instead of investing in academic excellence, universities often pour resources into sports facilities and programs that, while popular, do little to enhance the educational experience.

The financial burden of these programs often falls on students through increased tuition and fees. Research indicates that universities with higher athletic spending tend to allocate less to academic programs, exacerbating the trade-offs (Vedder, 2021). Critics argue that these funds would be better spent on initiatives directly impacting student success, such as faculty development, academic advising, and modernized instructional resources. Unless institutions realign their priorities, the core mission of higher education—preparing students for a competitive and innovative future—they will continue to suffer.

The Broader Consequences of Misplaced Priorities

The outsized focus on athletics reflects a cultural shift that frames higher education as an entertainment-driven enterprise rather than a space for intellectual growth. While sports can foster school spirit and community, their prioritization risks distorting the core mission of universities. This misalignment has far-reaching consequences, including diminished academic quality, inequities in resource allocation, and increased financial strain on students and families.

If universities are to reclaim their educational purpose, they must critically examine their budgets and values. By shifting resources from athletics and luxury amenities back to classrooms and laboratories, higher education can better serve its students and society. The choice is clear: prioritize learning and innovation or risk becoming little more than entertainment hubs with diminishing academic returns.

While the rise of non-academic administrators has undoubtedly increased the operational complexity of modern universities, it has also paved the way for shifting institutional priorities. This shift is perhaps most evident in the growing focus on non-academic endeavors, including the pursuit of prestige through athletics and luxury amenities. These priorities not only strain budgets but also risk diluting the core mission of higher education. To fully understand the impact of these misaligned priorities, it is crucial to examine how the sports arms race and the amenities-driven campus culture further exacerbate the challenges of administrative bloat.

The Rise of Non-Academic Administrators and Their Influence

The proliferation of non-academic administrators in higher education is a phenomenon that has reshaped the structure and priorities of colleges and universities. From 1987 to 2012, administrative positions in higher education grew by 60%, outpacing the growth of faculty positions and student enrollment (Desrochers & Kirshstein, 2014).

These positions, which include roles in student affairs, compliance, marketing, admissions, and diversity initiatives, reflect the increasing complexity of running a modern university. However, this rapid expansion raises concerns about efficiency, priorities, and the financial sustainability of higher education.

The rise of non-academic administrators is partly a response to external pressures. Regulatory compliance has grown more burdensome as federal and state governments impose requirements related to financial aid, campus safety, and equity. Institutions have hired administrators to navigate these regulations, ensuring that they remain eligible for government funding and avoid legal liabilities. For example, the Department of Education's Title IX mandates have led to the creation of compliance offices dedicated to addressing sexual harassment and gender equity issues.

Enrollment management has also driven administrative growth. Institutions now employ teams of specialists to develop recruitment strategies, optimize financial aid packages, and market their campuses to prospective students. These professionals focus on maximizing tuition revenue, often targeting out-of-state and international students who pay higher rates. While these efforts contribute to institutional budgets, they also reflect a shift from education as a public good to a revenue-driven enterprise (Ginsberg, 2011).

Another factor is the increased focus on student support services. Recognizing the diverse needs of today's students, colleges have expanded mental health counseling, career advising, disability services, and recreational activities. While these services are valuable, their expansion has significantly increased operational budgets. Critics argue that this emphasis on student experience sometimes prioritizes superficial metrics, such as satisfaction surveys, over academic rigor and outcomes.

The financial implications of administrative bloat are profound. High-level administrators, such as provosts, vice presidents, and deans, often earn salaries that far exceed those of faculty. For example, university presidents at major institutions frequently earn over $1 million annually, a stark contrast to the stagnating wages of adjunct and tenure-track professors. As administrative spending grows, it often comes at the expense of academic budgets, leading to larger class sizes, fewer course offerings, and overburdened faculty (Vedder, 2021).

Moreover, the expansion of administrative influence has diluted the role of faculty in institutional governance. Historically, faculty senates played a central role in shaping academic policies and priorities. However, as decision-making power has shifted to administrators, faculty input is increasingly sidelined. This trend, known as "managerialism," has transformed universities into hierarchical organizations where financial and marketing goals often overshadow educational missions (Duderstadt, 2000).

A further issue is the absence of many administrators, from directors and deans to assistant and associate vice presidents, vice presidents, and others, from the day-to-day operations of their institutions. Often, these individuals are visible only when opportunities for photo ops or resume-building activities arise, such as cutting ribbons at campus events. This practice reflects a culture of self-promotion over genuine institutional engagement, frequently resulting in career advancement for the administrators while leaving faculty and staff to shoulder the operational burdens. The resulting inefficiencies exacerbate the disconnect between administrative priorities and the actual needs of students and academic programs, further undermining the educational mission of higher education institutions. I strongly resonate with and believe in this powerful statement that perfectly describes these absentee, overpaid administrators:

Focus on Amenities Over Academics: Climbing Walls and Luxury Dorms

In an era of heightened competition for student enrollment, colleges and universities have increasingly prioritized amenities designed to attract prospective students. From climbing walls and lazy rivers to gourmet dining halls and luxury dormitories, these investments aim to create a campus lifestyle that appeals to affluent families. However, these expenditures often come at the expense of academic priorities, contributing to rising tuition costs without necessarily improving educational outcomes.

The focus on amenities stems from the perception that higher education is not only an academic endeavor but also a consumer product. Colleges market themselves as desirable places to live and socialize, emphasizing their campus facilities in promotional materials. This trend has been particularly pronounced at public universities, which compete for out-of-state and international students who pay higher tuition rates. For example, the University of Missouri built a $75 million student center featuring a spa, game room, and luxury furnishings, justifying the expense as essential for recruitment (Jacob et al., 2013).

These investments reflect a broader shift in the priorities of higher education institutions. Rather than focusing on academic excellence, many colleges allocate resources to non-essential luxuries that enhance campus aesthetics but do little to support student learning. For instance, while universities spend millions on athletic facilities and recreational spaces, academic departments often face budget cuts, hiring freezes, and outdated equipment. This misalignment undermines the primary mission of higher education: to provide quality instruction and foster intellectual growth.

The consequences of this trend are far-reaching. Amenities-driven spending exacerbates tuition increases, as the costs of constructing and maintaining these facilities are passed on to students. Research shows that institutions with higher levels of spending on amenities often have lower levels of spending on academics, highlighting a troubling trade-off (Jacob et al., 2013). Moreover, the focus on luxury facilities disproportionately benefits affluent students, who are more likely to prioritize lifestyle amenities, while low-income students bear the financial burden without enjoying equivalent benefits.

Critics argue that resources devoted to amenities could be better spent on initiatives that directly impact student success. For example, investments in faculty hiring, academic advising, and library resources have a proven impact on graduation rates and post-college outcomes. By contrast, the marginal benefits of climbing walls and gourmet dining remain unclear, raising questions about the sustainability of this spending model (Vedder, 2021).

Case Studies of Budget Mismanagement

The consequences of administrative bloat and amenities-driven spending are vividly illustrated through case studies of budget mismanagement. These examples reveal how misplaced priorities can undermine institutional missions and erode public trust in higher education.

Case Study 1: The University of California System

The University of California (UC) system, one of the most prestigious public university networks in the United States, has faced significant scrutiny for its administrative spending practices and budgetary decisions. A 2017 state audit revealed that the UC Office of the President, which oversees the system's ten campuses, had accumulated a $175 million reserve fund while simultaneously raising tuition for students and reducing funding for academic programs (California State Auditor, 2017). This revelation drew widespread criticism from students, faculty, and policymakers, who questioned the ethical and practical implications of these financial practices.

The audit highlighted that administrative spending within the UC system had increased by 28% over a four-year period, a rate far exceeding the growth in academic spending during the same timeframe. This finding amplified concerns that resources were being funneled into non-academic areas at the expense of teaching, research, and student support. For example, faculty reported difficulties securing funding for critical academic initiatives, while students experienced larger class sizes and reduced access to courses needed for timely graduation. The perception that administrative priorities were taking precedence over the system's educational mission sparked public outcry and led to demands for greater transparency and accountability.

One of the most contentious aspects of the audit was the UC Office of the President's justification for the reserve fund. Administrators argued that the fund was necessary to ensure financial stability, particularly in the face of fluctuating state funding and economic uncertainty. However, critics contended that the fund was poorly managed and lacked sufficient oversight. The audit revealed that the Office of the President had not disclosed the existence of the reserve fund to the UC Board of Regents or the state legislature, raising questions about transparency and governance. This lack of accountability eroded public trust and prompted calls for independent oversight of the system's financial practices.

The controversy also underscored broader issues of misaligned priorities within the UC system. While administrative budgets ballooned, academic programs faced significant challenges. Faculty positions remained unfilled, research funding stagnated, and student support services were under-resourced. Additionally, the decision to raise tuition—a move that disproportionately affected low- and middle-income students—was widely viewed as a failure to prioritize affordability and accessibility. This decision stood in stark contrast to the UC system's historical commitment to serving as a model of high-quality, affordable public education.

In response to the audit, the UC system implemented several measures aimed at improving transparency and financial oversight. These included greater scrutiny of administrative budgets, the creation of detailed financial reports, and increased engagement with the Board of Regents. However, the long-term effectiveness of these measures remains uncertain, as the systemic pressures driving administrative growth—such as compliance demands, enrollment management, and fundraising initiatives—continue to strain institutional resources.

The UC system's spending practices exemplify the challenges faced by large, publicly funded universities in balancing financial sustainability with their core academic mission. While the accumulation of reserve funds may be seen as prudent in some contexts, the lack of transparency and prioritization of administrative growth over academic investment highlights the need for robust oversight and a renewed focus on the foundational values of public higher education. As institutions nationwide grapple with similar issues, the lessons from the UC case underscore the importance of aligning financial decisions with the educational mission and values that define the role of public universities in society.

Case Study 2: The University of Akron

The University of Akron offers a compelling example of budget mismanagement and misplaced priorities, particularly regarding the allocation of resources toward athletics at the expense of academics. In the mid-2010s, the university faced a series of financial challenges, including declining enrollment and budget deficits. Rather than addressing these issues through strategic investments in academic programs or student support services, the administration chose to focus on high-cost, non-academic initiatives. Chief among these was the construction of a $61.7 million football stadium, a decision that sparked widespread criticism and unrest among students, faculty, and the broader community (Rogers, 2018).

The decision to invest in athletics despite financial instability exemplified a broader trend in higher education, where universities disproportionately prioritize sports programs to enhance institutional branding and alumni engagement. Proponents of such investments argue that athletics can bolster school spirit, attract prospective students, and encourage alumni donations. However, in the case of the University of Akron, these outcomes failed to materialize. Attendance at football games remained low, and the program did not generate sufficient revenue to justify its costs. Instead, the university faced mounting debt, forcing it to make cuts in other areas.

While the stadium project progressed, the University of Akron eliminated dozens of academic programs, including those in foreign languages, art history, and theater, arguing that these cuts were necessary to address financial shortfalls. Faculty layoffs followed, exacerbating tensions on campus and raising concerns about the institution's commitment to its core mission of education and research. Students, too, felt the impact of these decisions, facing reduced course offerings, larger class sizes, and diminished opportunities for intellectual and creative engagement. The contrast between the lavish investment in athletics and the austerity measures in academics fueled widespread backlash and damaged the university's reputation.

The broader implications of this case highlight the challenges and risks associated with prioritizing athletics over academics in higher education. While college sports can be a source of pride and identity for institutions, the financial realities of maintaining competitive athletic programs often undermine their purported benefits. For universities like Akron, which lack the national prominence and lucrative television contracts of powerhouse athletic programs, these investments are particularly risky. Research consistently shows that only a small fraction of collegiate athletic programs are profitable, and most require significant subsidies from institutional budgets (Vedder, 2021).

Critics argue that investments like Akron's stadium reflect a misalignment of priorities in higher education. The resources allocated to athletics could have been used to strengthen academic programs, recruit and retain faculty, or expand student support services. Instead, the emphasis on athletics diverted attention and funding from the university's core mission, leaving long-term academic and financial challenges unresolved. The situation also raises broader questions about the role of athletics in higher education, particularly at institutions that are not part of the elite ranks of collegiate sports.

In the aftermath of these decisions, the University of Akron has struggled to recover from the financial and reputational damage. Enrollment continued to decline, exacerbating budget deficits and limiting the university's ability to reinvest in academic programs. The case underscores the dangers of prioritizing short-term, high-profile projects over sustainable investments in education and student success. For institutions grappling with similar challenges, the lessons from Akron highlight the need for careful financial stewardship and a renewed focus on aligning institutional priorities with the educational mission of higher education.

Case Study 3: Claremont Colleges

The Claremont Colleges consortium, known for its prestigious liberal arts institutions, exemplifies how even elite private colleges are not immune to the issues of administrative bloat and resource misallocation. Pomona College, one of the most prominent members of the consortium, has faced criticism for its disproportionate administrative spending relative to its student population. A 2018 report revealed that Pomona employed more than 600 non-faculty staff members to support a student body of fewer than 1,700—a ratio that significantly exceeds national averages for higher education institutions (Eide, 2018).

Proponents of this administrative model argue that it reflects Pomona's commitment to providing an exceptional student experience. The extensive administrative staff supports a wide range of services, including mental health counseling, diversity and inclusion initiatives, career advising, and extracurricular programming. These services undoubtedly enhance certain aspects of campus life and contribute to the college's reputation for individualized attention and comprehensive support. However, critics contend that this level of administrative staffing raises significant concerns about financial sustainability and the efficient use of institutional resources.

The financial implications of such administrative expansion are considerable. Pomona's administrative salaries and overhead costs represent a substantial portion of its annual budget, diverting funds that could otherwise be allocated to academic priorities, such as faculty hiring, research support, and financial aid. While Pomona's large endowment allows it to absorb these costs more readily than public institutions or less affluent private colleges, the trend raises questions about the long-term sustainability of such spending, particularly in an era of increasing scrutiny over tuition costs and institutional accountability.

The administrative growth at Pomona also reflects broader trends in higher education, where institutions are investing heavily in non-academic services to meet evolving student expectations and regulatory demands. For example, the rising emphasis on diversity, equity, and inclusion has led many colleges to expand their administrative offices in these areas. While these initiatives are important, their rapid growth often outpaces the expansion of academic programs, leading to concerns about the balance of institutional priorities.

Moreover, the administrative-to-student ratio at Pomona highlights the growing influence of managerialism in higher education. As colleges and universities adopt increasingly corporate models of governance, decision-making often shifts away from faculty and toward administrators. This trend can undermine the academic mission of institutions, as managerial priorities, such as branding, rankings, and student satisfaction metrics, take precedence over intellectual rigor and scholarly pursuits (Ginsberg, 2011).

The example of Pomona College underscores the need for greater transparency and accountability in administrative spending, even at well-funded private institutions. While the Claremont Colleges are financially stable, the allocation of resources raises important questions about the role of administration in higher education and the potential trade-offs between student services and academic priorities. For smaller colleges with less robust endowments, adopting similar administrative models could pose significant financial risks, potentially exacerbating tuition increases and undermining the accessibility of higher education.

In the context of higher education reform, the case of Pomona College illustrates the importance of striking a balance between administrative growth and academic investment. Institutions must ensure that their administrative structures support, rather than overshadow, their educational missions. By prioritizing transparency, efficiency, and alignment with institutional values, colleges can address the challenges of administrative bloat while maintaining their commitment to student success and academic excellence.

Case Study 4: Clemson University

Clemson University, a public land-grant institution in South Carolina, provides another example of administrative expansion and resource mismanagement that has drawn scrutiny in recent years. Known for its competitive athletics program and commitment to student life, Clemson has faced criticism for prioritizing branding and amenities over academics, leading to significant financial and institutional challenges.

A major point of contention at Clemson has been its aggressive investment in athletics, particularly its nationally renowned football program. Between 2010 and 2020, Clemson spent more than $200 million on athletic facilities, including a $55 million football operations complex featuring a bowling alley, miniature golf course, and nap room (USA Today, 2019). Proponents argue that these investments enhance the university's visibility, attract top-tier athletes, and boost alumni engagement. However, critics contend that such expenditures reflect a troubling misalignment of priorities, especially as academic departments face resource constraints.

Simultaneously, Clemson has experienced significant administrative growth, with the number of non-academic staff members increasing substantially over the past decade. Administrative positions related to enrollment management, marketing, and student services have expanded, contributing to rising operational costs. In 2022, Clemson's administrative spending as a percentage of total expenditures exceeded the national average for public universities, prompting concerns about efficiency and the diversion of funds from academics (Higher Education Financial Trends Report, 2023).

While Clemson has also invested in luxury amenities for students, such as high-end dormitories and recreational facilities, these expenditures have contributed to rising tuition and fees. Between 2010 and 2020, tuition at Clemson increased by 42%, outpacing inflation and putting financial strain on students and families. Despite these increases, academic programs have faced challenges, including larger class sizes, limited course availability, and stagnant faculty hiring. Faculty members have expressed frustration over the perceived prioritization of athletics and administration over academic excellence, arguing that such decisions undermine the university's core mission (Clemson Faculty Senate Report, 2022).

The university's approach to fundraising has also drawn criticism. Clemson aggressively markets its brand to out-of-state and international students, who pay significantly higher tuition rates than in-state residents. While this strategy has bolstered revenue, it has raised concerns about equity and access for South Carolina residents, the primary beneficiaries of the land-grant mission. Additionally, some donors have expressed dissatisfaction with the allocation of funds, questioning whether their contributions are being used to enhance academics or simply to sustain the university's emphasis on athletics and amenities.

Clemson's practices highlight broader challenges faced by public universities in balancing their commitments to academic excellence, financial sustainability, and public service. While athletics and amenities can enhance institutional prestige and student experience, their disproportionate prioritization risks undermining the accessibility and quality of education. For Clemson, the emphasis on building its brand through athletics and luxury facilities has sparked debates about the proper allocation of resources at a land-grant institution tasked with serving the public good.

To address these issues, Clemson must reevaluate its budgetary priorities, ensuring that investments in athletics and administration do not come at the expense of academics. Greater transparency in financial decision-making, along with a renewed focus on supporting faculty and students, will be essential to restoring balance and reaffirming the university's educational mission. As a case study, Clemson underscores the importance of aligning institutional spending with the core values and responsibilities of public higher education.

Many administrators in higher education treat their current roles as mere stepping stones to higher positions, prioritizing self-promotion and career advancement over fulfilling their responsibilities. This pattern is evident in case studies such as the University of California system, where administrative spending ballooned while academic funding lagged, and the University of Akron, where decisions prioritized athletics over academics. Similarly, at Clemson University, investments in athletics and luxury amenities overshadowed academic priorities, while Pomona College's disproportionate administrative spending highlighted inefficiencies even in elite institutions. These examples illustrate how administrators often neglect the duties of their current positions, focusing instead on opportunities to bolster their resumes or gain visibility for the next career move. This approach not only compromises the institution's mission but also imposes significant costs on students and taxpayers, delivering little value in return. To address this, higher education institutions must ensure accountability, prioritize academic and student needs, and shift the focus from personal ambition to institutional effectiveness.

The rise of administrative bloat and the prioritization of amenities over academics have reshaped the financial and operational landscape of higher education. While some administrative growth and facility enhancements are necessary to meet modern challenges, their unchecked expansion often undermines the core mission of colleges and universities: education and research. Misaligned priorities, as illustrated by cases of budget mismanagement, erode public trust and contribute to rising tuition costs that burden students and families. Addressing these challenges requires a recommitment to transparency, efficiency, and the primacy of academic excellence, ensuring that higher education fulfills its promise as a public good.

At community colleges, administrators often emphasize that research is not part of the institution's mission, boasting about their focus on teaching over scholarly pursuits. While this perspective might seem student-centered, it inadvertently creates an environment where faculty are often disconnected from current developments in their fields. Without active engagement in research or ongoing professional development, faculty risk becoming outdated in their knowledge and underprepared to effectively teach students who aspire to transfer to universities. As a result, students transitioning from community colleges frequently struggle to compete with their university peers, who benefit from faculty immersed in cutting-edge research and industry practices. This academic gap contributes to higher rates of drop-outs and stop-outs among transfer students, undermining the community college's role as a stepping stone to higher educational success. To address this, community colleges must strike a balance by encouraging faculty to stay current in their fields while maintaining their teaching focus, ensuring students are better equipped for university-level challenges.

The unchecked rise of administrative bloat and the prioritization of luxury amenities over academics represent a critical misstep in higher education's evolution. These trends have diverted resources from teaching and research, undermining the core mission of colleges and universities while contributing to skyrocketing tuition and student debt. As case studies of budget mismanagement demonstrate, these misplaced priorities erode public trust and exacerbate inequities, leaving students and faculty to bear the consequences of institutional misalignment. To reclaim higher education's promise as a pathway to opportunity and intellectual growth, colleges must refocus on transparency, accountability, and academic excellence. The future of higher education depends not on climbing walls or corporate-style management but on a renewed commitment to learning, innovation, and the pursuit of knowledge as a public good, ensuring a sustainable and equitable path forward for students and society.

Chapter 6

The Erosion of Academic Quality

The erosion of academic quality in higher education signals a profound shift in the mission and values of institutions once dedicated to intellectual rigor and societal advancement. What was historically a pursuit of critical thinking and transformative learning has increasingly become a system driven by market forces, financial metrics, and superficial benchmarks. Profit-driven programs prioritize revenue over substance, adjunct faculty are overworked and undervalued, and grade inflation compromises the integrity of degrees. As colleges and universities navigate these pressures, the true cost is borne by students, who face diluted educational experiences and diminished opportunities. This chapter examines the forces undermining academic quality and explores the urgent need to realign higher education with its foundational purpose of cultivating knowledge, critical inquiry, and meaningful achievement.

The Shift Toward Profit-Driven Programs and Away from Rigorous Education

The prioritization of profit-driven programs over rigorous academic education has significantly transformed the mission of higher education institutions in the United States. Financial pressures, changing student demographics, and market demands have incentivized colleges and universities to design programs that generate revenue, often at the expense of academic rigor and intellectual depth. This shift is evident in the growing emphasis on vocational and professional programs—such as business, healthcare, and technology—while liberal arts disciplines, which traditionally prioritize critical thinking and ethical reasoning, experience funding cuts and declining enrollments (Bok, 2003).

A primary driver of this transformation is the increasing cost of higher education. Rising tuition and living expenses have made students and families prioritize degrees with clear, high-paying career outcomes. In response, institutions have heavily marketed programs perceived as lucrative, often designing curricula that cater to market trends rather than foundational knowledge. For instance, many universities have reduced general education requirements to streamline degrees and make them more appealing to students seeking a faster, career-focused path (Hersh & Keeling, 2013).

However, the role of general education courses as a revenue generator cannot be overlooked. These courses, often taught in large lecture halls or online formats with minimal instructor involvement, are a significant source of income for institutions while adding little to the overall education of the student. Critics argue that this system prioritizes financial gain over meaningful intellectual development, treating students as revenue streams rather than individuals pursuing holistic education. As a result, many students graduate with a sense that these courses were little more than hurdles, rather than opportunities to broaden their perspectives or develop transferable skills.

Moreover, the use of general education courses to sustain degrees with limited employability must be reevaluated and ultimately stopped. Institutions should instead focus on designing curricula that emphasize the core, required courses for useful and practical majors. By streamlining programs to prioritize relevant and applicable knowledge, colleges and universities can better prepare students for the demands of the workforce and reduce the financial burden of superfluous coursework. This shift would ensure that higher education fulfills its promise of equipping students with skills and qualifications that translate into meaningful careers, rather than perpetuating outdated models that serve institutional interests at the expense of student success.

For-profit colleges epitomize the dangers of profit-driven education. These institutions often emphasize enrollment growth over academic quality, using aggressive marketing tactics to attract students while offering programs with minimal academic oversight. Many for-profit colleges have faced lawsuits and closures due to their inability to provide students with the promised return on investment, such as marketable skills or employment opportunities (Cellini & Turner, 2019). Even nonprofit institutions are not immune to this trend. Public and private colleges increasingly use corporate-style management strategies, prioritizing programs that enhance their financial standing or improve their rankings, sometimes at the expense of core academic values.

This focus on profit-driven programming also undermines faculty autonomy and academic freedom. Programs designed with marketability in mind often impose restrictions on faculty in terms of course content and grading standards. Additionally, tenure-track positions are being replaced with contingent roles that emphasize student satisfaction and retention, further weakening the balance between rigorous education and institutional financial goals (Kezar et al., 2019).

The long-term consequences of this trend are profound. While market-driven programs may provide students with immediate job opportunities, they often fail to equip them with the critical thinking and problem-solving skills necessary for long-term success in a rapidly changing economy. Moreover, the devaluation of liberal arts education threatens to erode the civic and cultural foundations of society, as fewer students engage with disciplines that foster democratic participation and global awareness.

Over-Reliance on Adjunct Faculty and Its Consequences for Teaching Quality

The growing reliance on adjunct faculty has become a defining feature of modern higher education, with profound implications for teaching quality, student outcomes, and institutional culture. Adjunct faculty—part-time, non-tenure-track instructors—now teach more than half of all undergraduate courses in the United States, a figure that reflects a significant shift in institutional hiring practices over the past several decades (American Federation of Teachers, 2020). While adjuncts bring valuable expertise and flexibility, their precarious working conditions limit their ability to provide high-quality education.

Adjunct faculty are often employed at a fraction of the cost of full-time, tenure-track professors. The average adjunct earns approximately $2,700 per course, with no benefits, job security, or opportunities for advancement. Many adjuncts teach at multiple institutions to make ends meet, a practice known as "freeway flying," which limits the time and energy they can devote to individual students (Kezar et al., 2019). Furthermore, adjuncts often lack access to resources such as office space, professional development, and academic advising, reducing their ability to engage meaningfully with students and contribute to institutional decision-making.

The over-reliance on adjuncts also has significant consequences for students. Research has shown that students taught by adjunct faculty are less likely to persist to graduation, particularly in their first year of college (Bettinger & Long, 2010). This disparity is attributed to the limited availability of adjuncts for mentoring, advising, and fostering long-term academic relationships. Adjuncts, who are often excluded from campus governance and curriculum planning, may also be less integrated into the academic community, further diminishing their ability to contribute to student success.

The adjunctification of higher education is a symptom of broader structural inequities within academia. While institutions save money by employing adjuncts, these savings are often redirected toward administrative growth and non-academic initiatives rather than reinvested in teaching or research. This trend reflects a troubling devaluation of teaching, as adjuncts, who shoulder a significant portion of instructional responsibilities, are denied the stability and support necessary to excel in their roles.

Addressing this issue requires systemic reform. Institutions must commit to improving compensation, benefits, and job security for adjunct faculty, while also creating pathways for professional development and advancement. By recognizing the vital contributions of adjuncts and providing them with the resources they need, colleges and universities can enhance teaching quality and foster a more equitable academic environment.

Grades and Graduations Tied to Funding

The increasing linkage between grades, graduation rates, and institutional funding has created significant challenges for maintaining academic quality. Performance-based funding models, which tie state funding to metrics such as graduation rates, retention rates, and job placement statistics, have become increasingly common in public higher education. While these policies are designed to improve accountability and incentivize student success, they have unintended consequences that undermine the integrity of academic standards (Hillman et al., 2015).

One of the primary effects of performance-based funding is the pressure it places on faculty and administrators to ensure high graduation rates. Faculty often report feeling pressured to inflate grades and reduce the rigor of coursework to improve student retention and progression. This dynamic creates a culture where academic standards are compromised to meet institutional goals, leading to the devaluation of degrees and credentials (Kelchen, 2018).

Institutions also implement strategies to streamline graduation pathways, such as reducing credit requirements for degrees or offering simplified course options. While these initiatives can help students complete their education more efficiently, they often come at the expense of intellectual depth and academic rigor. For example, some institutions have shifted away from requiring capstone projects, comprehensive exams, or other high-impact learning experiences, prioritizing metrics over meaningful educational outcomes.

The focus on performance metrics also exacerbates inequities among institutions. Colleges and universities serving disadvantaged populations often face greater challenges in meeting funding criteria, as their students may require additional support to succeed. Without adequate resources, these institutions risk losing funding, further limiting their ability to provide a high-quality education and perpetuating cycles of inequality (Hillman et al., 2015).

To address these issues, policymakers and institutions must develop funding models that prioritize quality over quantity. This includes incorporating qualitative assessments of student learning and providing resources to support underserved populations. By aligning funding mechanisms with the core mission of higher education, institutions can ensure that accountability measures enhance, rather than erode, academic quality.

Grade Inflation and the Decline of Academic Standards

Grade inflation, or the gradual increase in average grades over time without a corresponding increase in student achievement, has become a pervasive issue in higher education. Studies show that the average GPA at American colleges and universities has risen steadily over the past five decades, with A grades now accounting for nearly half of all grades awarded (Rojstaczer & Healy, 2012). This trend, while sometimes attributed to better-prepared students, is largely driven by institutional pressures that prioritize student satisfaction and retention over rigorous evaluation.

One of the key drivers of grade inflation is the reliance on student evaluations in faculty performance reviews. Faculty members often feel pressured to award higher grades to avoid negative feedback, which can affect their job security and opportunities for promotion. This is particularly true for adjunct faculty, who are more vulnerable to poor evaluations and administrative oversight (Kezar et al., 2019). Additionally, institutions seeking to maintain enrollment and improve graduation rates may encourage leniency in grading practices, creating a culture where high grades are expected rather than earned.

The consequences of grade inflation are far-reaching. Inflated grades undermine the value of academic credentials, making it difficult for employers and graduate schools to assess the true capabilities of candidates. This devaluation contributes to skepticism about the quality of higher education and diminishes the motivation of students to engage deeply with their coursework. Furthermore, grade inflation exacerbates inequities, as students from institutions with more rigorous grading standards may face disadvantages in competitive job markets or graduate admissions (Rojstaczer & Healy, 2012).

Addressing grade inflation requires a cultural shift within academia. Institutions must support faculty in maintaining rigorous grading standards and develop alternative measures of accountability that do not compromise academic quality. Transparency in grading practices, combined with efforts to realign institutional priorities, can help restore the integrity of higher education and ensure that degrees reflect meaningful achievement.

The erosion of academic quality in higher education is not just an institutional failure; it is a societal challenge with profound implications for the future. The shift toward profit-driven programs, reliance on underpaid adjunct faculty, grade inflation, and performance-based funding has compromised the integrity of learning and undermined the transformative power of education. If colleges and universities are to fulfill their mission as engines of knowledge and social progress, they must recommit to academic rigor, equitable practices, and a student-centered approach that values intellectual growth over financial metrics. The future of higher education—and the broader society it serves—depends on the courage to confront these challenges and restore education as a force for innovation, equity, and enlightenment.

Chapter 7

Diverging Purposes of Colleges and Universities

The diverging purposes of colleges and universities reveal a growing divide in the mission, priorities, and outcomes of higher education institutions. While universities focus on research, publishing, and grant acquisition to solidify their status as global knowledge hubs, colleges champion open access and workforce development, often serving as the gateway to education for marginalized communities. This duality highlights both the strengths and tensions within the higher education system: universities drive innovation but often disconnect from real-world applications, while colleges provide practical training yet struggle with resource limitations and societal undervaluation. These contrasting missions have profound implications for students, who navigate mismatched priorities, inequities, and structural inefficiencies in pursuit of their aspirations. This chapter examines the complex interplay between colleges and universities, exploring the hierarchy, cultural biases, and systemic challenges that shape the future of higher education.

Universities: The Research-Driven Model

Universities have long been revered as hubs of intellectual discovery and innovation, playing a critical role in advancing knowledge and addressing societal challenges. Historically, these institutions were established to cultivate thinkers, leaders, and innovators who could contribute to the greater good. In the modern era, this mission has evolved into a high-stakes, research-driven model characterized by a relentless focus on publishing, securing grants, and achieving global prestige. While this model has spurred groundbreaking advancements and positioned universities as leaders in innovation, it has also created significant tensions within higher education, raising questions about the balance between research priorities, teaching, and student engagement.

At the heart of the research-driven model is the pursuit of publication and grant funding. Faculty members at research universities are often evaluated based on their ability to publish in high-impact journals and secure external grants, which serve as critical metrics for tenure, promotion, and institutional rankings. This "publish or perish" culture incentivizes academics to prioritize research output, often at the expense of teaching and mentorship. As a result, undergraduate education can take a backseat, with many courses taught by adjuncts or graduate students, leaving undergraduates with fewer opportunities to interact with experienced faculty (Bok, 2003).

The emphasis on grant acquisition has further reshaped the priorities of research universities. External funding from federal agencies, private corporations, and philanthropic organizations provides vital resources for large-scale research projects, but it also creates disparities within academia. STEM fields, which attract significant grant funding, often receive preferential treatment in terms of resources and infrastructure, while disciplines in the humanities and social sciences struggle to secure adequate support. This imbalance not only marginalizes certain academic fields but also narrows the scope of research to areas with immediate commercial or societal applications (Schulz, 2020).

Despite its many successes, the research-driven model has unintended consequences that undermine the broader mission of higher education.

One of the most significant challenges is the growing disconnect between academic research and real-world application. While universities are responsible for producing a wealth of knowledge, much of it remains confined to academic journals and conferences, inaccessible to policymakers, practitioners, or the general public. This "ivory tower" perception diminishes the societal impact of research, particularly in fields where actionable insights could address pressing global challenges, such as climate change, public health, and social inequality (Stokes, 1997).

The relentless focus on research also affects faculty workload and well-being. The pressure to publish, secure grants, and maintain a high academic profile often leads to burnout, reduced job satisfaction, and a diminished ability to engage with students. Furthermore, the competitive nature of grant funding fosters an environment where collaboration can be deprioritized in favor of individual success, hindering the interdisciplinary approaches needed to tackle complex problems.

However, the research-driven model is not without its benefits. Universities have been at the forefront of technological and scientific breakthroughs that have transformed society. From advances in medicine and renewable energy to the development of artificial intelligence, university research has addressed some of the most critical challenges of our time. Moreover, the emphasis on research fosters an environment of intellectual curiosity and exploration, attracting top talent from around the world and enriching academic communities.

To address the tensions within the research-driven model, universities must strike a better balance between research priorities and teaching responsibilities. Greater recognition and support for teaching excellence, coupled with incentives for faculty to engage with students, can help restore the educational mission of higher education. Additionally, fostering stronger connections between academic research and societal needs through public engagement, interdisciplinary collaboration, and translational research initiatives can bridge the gap between theory and practice.

The research-driven model has cemented universities' roles as engines of innovation and progress, but it must evolve to meet the diverse demands of higher education in the 21st century. By aligning research priorities with the needs of students, communities, and society at large, universities can fulfill their dual mission of advancing knowledge and preparing the next generation of leaders and innovators.

Focus on Research, Publishing, and Grant Acquisition

Universities, especially research-intensive institutions, are heavily focused on advancing knowledge through research, publishing, and securing external funding. This emphasis aligns with their mission to drive innovation, address societal challenges, and maintain global competitiveness. Faculty at these institutions are often evaluated primarily on their research output, including the number of publications, citations, and grants acquired. This "publish or perish" culture incentivizes faculty to prioritize research activities, often at the expense of teaching and student engagement (Bok, 2003).

Research universities play a critical role in scientific and technological advancements. Federal agencies such as the National Institutes of Health (NIH) and the National Science Foundation (NSF) fund projects that lead to breakthroughs in medicine, engineering, and environmental science. However, the competition for these grants creates disparities within academia. Departments and disciplines that attract significant funding, such as STEM fields, receive substantial institutional support, while others, like the humanities, struggle to secure resources (Schulz, 2020).

The emphasis on grant acquisition also drives universities to adopt a corporate-like structure. Administrative offices dedicated to grant writing, compliance, and research management have expanded significantly, increasing operational costs. Critics argue that this model shifts the focus from education to revenue generation, creating a disconnection between institutional priorities and the needs of students (Altbach, 2011).

Overproduction of PhD degrees and Its Impact on the Job Market

The coveted PhD has been watered down by the proliferation of low-quality doctorates such as the EdD, and even the conversion of EdDs into PhDs that require no dissertation but instead a capstone paper of only 40 to 50 pages. This stands in stark contrast to a traditional dissertation, which typically spans over 200 pages and involves at least two years of intensive research. Doctoral-granting universities are capitalizing on these diluted doctoral programs as revenue streams.

The significant growth in PhD production over recent decades has saturated the academic job market, leaving many doctoral graduates underemployed or unable to secure tenure-track positions. Between 2000 and 2020, the number of PhDs awarded in the United States increased by 45%, while tenure-track opportunities remained stagnant or even declined (National Science Foundation, 2021). This imbalance between supply and demand has led to a surge in precarious adjunct positions, where highly educated individuals are employed on short-term contracts with low pay and minimal benefits.

The repercussions of this oversupply extend beyond academia. Many PhD graduates struggle to transition into industry roles due to the highly specialized nature of their training, which often does not align with workforce demands. Even those who secure non-academic employment frequently face difficulties in demonstrating the value of their research skills to employers, leading to underemployment and job dissatisfaction (Sauermann & Roach, 2012).

This overproduction of PhDs also impacts universities. The influx of highly qualified candidates enables institutions to rely heavily on contingent labor for teaching and research, perpetuating a cycle of low pay and job insecurity. Addressing these systemic issues requires a reevaluation of graduate education, including limiting PhD enrollment, expanding career training, and aligning programs with diverse career trajectories.

The Disconnect Between Academic Research and Real-World Application

A persistent critique of research universities is the perceived gap between academic research and its practical applications. While universities are hubs of innovation, much of the knowledge they produce remains confined to academic journals and conferences, inaccessible to policymakers, practitioners, or the general public. This "ivory tower" perception undermines the societal relevance of university research, particularly in fields where actionable insights could address pressing challenges, such as climate change, public health, and social justice (Stokes, 1997).

The emphasis on basic research over applied research contributes to this disconnect. While basic research is essential for long-term innovation, it often lacks immediate practical outcomes, leading to criticism that universities prioritize theoretical knowledge over real-world impact. Bridging this gap requires fostering interdisciplinary collaborations, engaging with external stakeholders, and promoting translational research that converts academic findings into tangible solutions.

Colleges: Accessibility and Workforce Development

Colleges, particularly community colleges (i.e. two-year institutions), serve as pillars of accessibility in higher education, offering opportunities to students from all walks of life. Their open-door admissions policies ensure that anyone seeking to improve their education, gain workforce skills, or prepare for transfer to a four-year institution can find a place to start. Beyond accessibility, colleges play a vital role in workforce development, aligning programs with local labor market needs to equip students with practical, in-demand skills. However, this dual mission of accessibility and workforce training often creates tension between addressing immediate economic demands and fostering broader educational goals like critical thinking and civic engagement. This section delves into the unique challenges and opportunities colleges face in balancing these competing priorities, the proliferation of short-term credentials, and their role as "transfer machines" navigating systemic barriers to student success.

Open Access to All Potential Students

Community colleges and two-year institutions are central to the democratization of higher education, offering open access to students from diverse backgrounds. Their inclusive admissions policies provide opportunities to individuals who might otherwise be excluded from postsecondary education due to academic or financial barriers. This model ensures that higher education is within reach for low-income students, first-generation college attendees, adult learners, and those seeking a second chance at education (Cohen et al., 2014). By accepting nearly all applicants, community colleges play a pivotal role in addressing systemic inequalities and promoting social mobility.

This open-access model serves as a critical lifeline for many students, particularly those who face socioeconomic or educational disadvantages. For example, adult learners returning to school to gain new skills or change careers find community colleges to be flexible and accommodating, offering evening, weekend, and online courses. Similarly, recent high school graduates who lack the academic credentials for university admission can begin their educational journey at a community college, building the skills and credits needed to transfer to a four-year institution. This inclusivity strengthens the workforce, fosters individual growth, and contributes to the broader economy by creating a more educated and skilled population.

However, open access also presents significant challenges for institutions and students alike. Many community college students enter with academic deficiencies, particularly in math and English, requiring remedial or developmental education before they can enroll in credit-bearing courses. Studies show that nearly two-thirds of community college students take at least one remedial course, with many spending multiple semesters in developmental education (Bailey et al., 2015). While these programs are essential for addressing gaps in knowledge, they can delay student progress and contribute to lower graduation rates. Students often become discouraged by the extended timeline, leading many to drop out before completing their degrees.

To address these challenges, community colleges must provide robust support systems that enable student success. Tutoring centers, writing labs, and peer mentoring programs can help students overcome academic hurdles. Comprehensive advising services can guide students through course selection and career planning, ensuring they stay on track to meet their goals. Financial aid support is equally crucial, as many community college students face significant economic challenges. Offering scholarships, grants, and work-study opportunities can reduce financial stress and increase retention.

Furthermore, community colleges must adopt innovative approaches to developmental education. Co-requisite models, which allow students to enroll in credit-bearing courses while receiving additional academic support, have shown promise in accelerating progress and improving outcomes. By balancing accessibility with targeted interventions, community colleges can maintain their commitment to open access while addressing the barriers that hinder student achievement.

Workforce Training vs. Liberal Arts Education: A Conflicting Mission

Community colleges often face a dual mission that reflects the complex needs of their students and communities. On one hand, they are tasked with providing workforce training programs that address local economic demands. These programs, which include fields such as healthcare, information technology, and skilled trades, prepare students for immediate employment by offering practical skills and certifications. Workforce development initiatives are particularly attractive to nontraditional students and those seeking short-term training to enter or reenter the labor market (Carnevale et al., 2012).

The success of workforce training programs has elevated their prominence within community colleges, leading to increased funding and enrollment. These programs align with regional workforce needs, ensuring that students gain marketable skills and meet employer expectations. For example, a community college in a region with a growing healthcare industry may offer programs in nursing, medical coding, and radiologic technology. These targeted efforts not only benefit students but also contribute to economic growth by supplying industries with a skilled labor force.

However, the growing emphasis on workforce training can overshadow the broader goals of liberal arts education. Liberal arts programs, which prioritize critical thinking, creativity, and civic engagement, are often perceived as less practical in a job-oriented educational landscape. Consequently, these programs struggle to attract students and secure funding, despite their long-term benefits. A liberal arts education equips students with transferable skills that are valuable across industries and fosters intellectual curiosity that extends beyond the workplace.

This tension between workforce training and liberal arts education highlights a fundamental challenge for community colleges: balancing immediate economic needs with broader educational goals. While workforce programs provide tangible benefits, an overemphasis on short-term outcomes risks narrowing the scope of education. Students may graduate with job-specific skills but lack the adaptability and problem-solving abilities required to navigate a rapidly changing labor market.

To address this conflict, community colleges must strive for a balanced approach. Integrating liberal arts principles into workforce programs can provide students with a well-rounded education that combines practical skills with critical thinking and communication abilities. For example, a nursing program could include courses on ethics, psychology, or sociology to prepare students for the complex interpersonal and ethical challenges they may face in their careers.

Similarly, offering interdisciplinary programs that bridge technical and liberal arts fields can attract students seeking both career readiness and intellectual growth.

The Proliferation of Certificates and Associate Degrees with Limited Value

The increasing popularity of short-term credentials, such as certificates and associate degrees, reflects the demand for quick and affordable pathways to employment. Community colleges have responded to this demand by expanding their offerings in fields like healthcare, business, and technology. These programs provide students with entry-level skills and certifications that allow them to join the workforce quickly, addressing labor shortages in high-demand industries. However, the economic returns of these credentials vary widely, raising concerns about their long-term value (Carnevale et al., 2012).

While some certificate holders see significant wage gains, particularly in high-skill fields like information technology or advanced manufacturing, others experience limited financial benefits. Research shows that certificate holders in low-wage sectors, such as retail or food service, often earn less than high school graduates, even with postsecondary credentials (Bailey et al., 2015). This disparity highlights the need for community colleges to carefully align their programs with labor market demands, ensuring that students receive credentials that lead to sustainable careers.

The focus on short-term credentials also risks creating a stratified education system that reinforces socioeconomic inequalities. Low-income and minority students, who are overrepresented in community colleges, are often funneled into certificate programs with limited upward mobility. These students may complete their education only to find that their credentials do not provide a meaningful wage premium or clear pathways to advancement. By contrast, students attending universities often have access to broader career opportunities and higher earning potential, creating a divide in outcomes based on the type of institution attended.

To address these disparities, community colleges must prioritize the quality and relevance of their credential offerings. Partnering with employers to design programs that align with industry standards can ensure that students gain skills that are in demand. Additionally, providing clear pathways for credential holders to pursue further education—such as stackable credentials that build toward associate or bachelor's degrees—can enhance their long-term career prospects.

Community colleges must also advocate for equitable funding and support for all students, regardless of their chosen pathway. While certificates and associate degrees offer valuable opportunities, they should not become a substitute for broader educational aspirations. By balancing the expansion of short-term credentials with a commitment to student mobility and lifelong learning, community colleges can fulfill their mission of providing accessible and meaningful education for all.

The "Transfer Machine" Model and Its Role in Student Attrition

Community colleges are often perceived as "transfer machines," designed to provide students with an affordable and accessible pathway to four-year universities. For many students, this model offers the promise of completing the first two years of a bachelor's degree at a lower cost before transitioning to a university to finish their education. However, the reality of the transfer process is fraught with systemic barriers that impede student progress and contribute to high rates of attrition. Credit loss, unclear articulation agreements, and limited advising support make transferring from community colleges to universities far more complex and costly than it should be.

One of the most significant challenges transfer students face is credit loss. Research indicates that, on average, students lose about 43% of their credits during the transfer process (Simone, 2014). This loss often results from a lack of alignment between community college and university curricula. Courses completed at a community college may not meet the requirements of a student's intended major at their transfer institution, forcing them to retake classes or enroll in additional courses to fulfill degree requirements. This inefficiency not only prolongs the time to graduation but also increases tuition costs, leaving students with higher levels of debt.

The lack of clear and consistent articulation agreements between two- and four-year institutions exacerbates these challenges. Articulation agreements are formal arrangements that outline how credits transfer from one institution to another, ensuring that courses taken at a community college align with the requirements of a bachelor's degree program. However, these agreements are often incomplete, outdated, or nonexistent, leaving students to navigate the transfer process without clear guidance. Even when agreements exist, they may not account for changes in university policies or new degree programs, creating confusion and uncertainty for students (Jenkins & Fink, 2015).

Advising, a critical component of the transfer process, is another area where systemic inefficiencies hinder student success. Many community colleges lack the resources to provide comprehensive transfer advising, leaving students unaware of the requirements for their intended bachelor's degree programs. Students often select courses without understanding how they will transfer or meet their future degree requirements, resulting in wasted time and resources. Limited advising support also means that students may not receive guidance on how to navigate the application process, financial aid opportunities, or the social and academic adjustments required for success at a four-year institution.

The consequences of these systemic barriers are stark. Nationally, only about 33% of community college students successfully transfer to a four-year university, and fewer than half of those who transfer go on to complete a bachelor's degree (Jenkins & Fink, 2015). This attrition reflects not a lack of student ability or ambition but rather the structural challenges embedded in the transfer process. For many students, these obstacles lead to frustration, extended timelines, and financial burdens that force them to abandon their educational goals altogether.

Addressing the inefficiencies of the "transfer machine" model requires a coordinated effort between community colleges and universities. Strengthening collaboration between institutions is essential to creating seamless transfer pathways that minimize credit loss and streamline the transition process. Comprehensive articulation agreements that clearly outline transferable credits and degree requirements can help ensure that students' coursework is recognized and valued. Additionally, shared advising systems that involve both community colleges and universities can provide students with consistent, accurate guidance throughout their educational journey.

Investing in enhanced support services for transfer students is also critical. Community colleges must prioritize transfer advising and provide students with the tools and resources needed to make informed decisions about their education. Universities, for their part, must commit to supporting transfer students once they arrive, offering orientation programs, mentoring, and academic support to help them adjust to the demands of a four-year institution.

Ultimately, reforming the transfer process is not just a matter of improving efficiency—it is a matter of equity. Community colleges serve a disproportionately large share of low-income, first-generation, and minority students, who rely on the transfer pathway to access affordable higher education and achieve upward mobility. By addressing the systemic barriers within the "transfer machine" model, colleges and universities can ensure that these students have a fair and equitable opportunity to reach their educational and career aspirations.

Universities vs. Colleges: The Hierarchy of Higher Education

The hierarchy of higher education in the United States reflects a deeply entrenched university-centric model that positions research universities as the pinnacle of academic achievement, while colleges—particularly community colleges—are relegated to a lower tier. This division stems from societal and cultural biases that equate universities with intellectual rigor, innovation, and prestige, and colleges with practicality, remedial education, or a stepping-stone to "real" higher education. While universities excel in producing groundbreaking research and theoretical knowledge, colleges fulfill equally critical roles as engines of accessibility, workforce development, and community engagement. Yet, the disparities in funding, societal recognition, and institutional priorities perpetuate inequities, marginalizing colleges and the students they serve.

One of the key consequences of this hierarchy is its impact on funding. Research universities often receive the lion's share of public and private financial support, including government grants, alumni donations, and corporate partnerships. Community colleges, by contrast, must often operate on lean budgets while serving larger and more diverse populations. These funding disparities reinforce the perception that universities are more valuable than colleges, even though community colleges play an essential role in promoting equity and economic mobility for underserved communities (Labaree, 2017).

This divide also affects students' perceptions and aspirations. Many students are conditioned to view universities as the ultimate goal of higher education, dismissing the opportunities and value that colleges offer. This perception influences enrollment decisions, with some students bypassing community colleges altogether, even when they might be the best fit financially and academically. Others enroll in colleges intending to transfer to a university but face systemic barriers, such as credit loss and institutional competition, that prolong their education and increase costs. Addressing these structural challenges requires not only systemic reform but also a cultural shift that values the unique contributions of both universities and colleges.

The Prestige Trap: How the University-Centric Model Undermines Colleges

The cultural emphasis on universities as "elite" institutions perpetuates a prestige trap that marginalizes community colleges and their essential contributions to higher education. This trap is rooted in societal narratives that prioritize research, selectivity, and rankings over accessibility, workforce development, and student-centered education.

These biases have significant implications for funding, public perception, and the equitable distribution of resources across the higher education landscape.

Public perceptions of prestige directly influence how funding is allocated. Universities often attract disproportionate public funding and private donations due to their perceived elite status, even as community colleges serve larger and more diverse student populations. For example, research universities frequently secure multimillion-dollar grants for specialized programs, while community colleges struggle to fund basic infrastructure improvements or expand student services. This disparity leaves community colleges under-resourced and underappreciated, despite their vital role in providing affordable education and vocational training (Labaree, 2017).

The prestige trap also affects the recognition of community colleges' achievements. While universities are celebrated for their research and innovation, the contributions of community colleges—such as improving economic mobility, addressing workforce gaps, and fostering social equity—are often overlooked or undervalued. This devaluation extends to students, who may feel stigmatized for attending community colleges, even when these institutions align better with their educational and career goals.

Breaking free from the prestige trap requires a reimagining of the higher education narrative. Community colleges must be recognized not as "lesser" institutions but as essential partners in the broader educational ecosystem. Policymakers, employers, and educational leaders should advocate for equitable funding, celebrate the unique successes of community colleges, and dismantle the cultural bias that equates prestige with selectivity rather than impact.

Degrees of Separation: Workforce-Ready vs. Research-Focused Education

The divide between workforce-ready education at colleges and research-focused education at universities underscores broader tensions in the priorities of higher education. Community colleges emphasize practical skills and job training, aligning their programs with local labor market demands to prepare students for immediate employment. Universities, on the other hand, focus on theoretical knowledge, research, and innovation, often prioritizing long-term intellectual advancement over immediate workforce needs. While both approaches are valuable, their misalignment creates challenges for students and institutions alike.

Colleges are increasingly seen as hubs for workforce development, offering certificate and associate degree programs in fields such as healthcare, information technology, and skilled trades. These programs are designed to provide students with the skills and credentials needed to secure well-paying jobs in high-demand industries. However, this workforce-ready model can sometimes overshadow broader educational goals, such as fostering critical thinking, creativity, and adaptability. Critics argue that this narrow focus risks creating a two-tiered education system, where college students are funneled into specific career tracks with limited upward mobility (Carnevale et al., 2012).

Universities, by contrast, prioritize research and theoretical exploration, often producing graduates with deep academic knowledge but limited practical skills. Employers frequently cite a gap between the competencies needed in the workplace and the abilities of university graduates, such as communication, problem-solving, and teamwork. This disconnect highlights the need for universities to incorporate more experiential learning and interdisciplinary approaches that bridge the gap between theory and practice (Carnevale et al., 2012).

Bridging the divide between these models requires greater collaboration and alignment of curricula. Colleges and universities must work together to create seamless educational pathways that combine the strengths of both approaches. For example, articulation agreements can ensure that workforce-ready credentials earned at colleges align with university degree programs, allowing students to build on their skills without losing credits or duplicating coursework. Additionally, partnerships with employers can inform program design at both types of institutions, ensuring that graduates are prepared to meet the evolving demands of the labor market.

By integrating workforce readiness with theoretical knowledge, colleges and universities can better serve students and society, fostering a higher education system that values both practical skills and intellectual growth. This collaborative approach not only enhances student success but also addresses the broader challenges of economic competitiveness and social equity.

The Transfer Bottleneck: A Broken Pathway to Success

For millions of students, transferring from a community college to a university is intended to be a cost-effective pathway to earning a bachelor's degree. However, the reality of the transfer process often creates significant barriers that cost students both time and money. Credit loss, mismatched curricula, inconsistent advising, and financial strain make this transition more challenging than it should be, leaving many students unable to complete their degrees or significantly delaying their progress.

One of the most common issues students face during the transfer process is credit loss. Studies show that on average, community college students lose 43% of their earned credits when transferring to a university (Simone, 2014). These losses occur due to mismatched curricula, differing course requirements, and a lack of alignment between two-year and four-year institutions. For example, a student might complete general education or major-specific courses at a community college, only to find that their new institution does not accept them as meeting degree requirements. This forces students to retake courses they have already completed, extending their time to graduation and increasing tuition and related expenses.

Mismatched curricula further complicate the transfer process. Community colleges and universities often operate with limited collaboration, leading to discrepancies in course content, credit requirements, and degree expectations. Without clear articulation agreements—formal agreements that specify how credits transfer between institutions—students are left navigating a maze of uncertainty. Even when such agreements exist, they may not account for changes in university policies, leaving students vulnerable to sudden shifts that invalidate their earned credits (Jenkins & Fink, 2015).

Financial challenges exacerbate these barriers. The extended timeline caused by credit loss and additional coursework increases the total cost of obtaining a degree. Students who planned on saving money by starting at a community college may end up paying significantly more than they anticipated, particularly if their financial aid eligibility runs out before completing their bachelor's degree. For low-income students, who make up a large percentage of community college attendees, these costs can be devastating, leading many to drop out entirely.

Institutional competition between colleges and universities further undermines the transfer process. Rather than collaborating to ensure seamless transitions, many institutions prioritize their own interests. Universities may resist accepting transfer credits to maximize the number of courses students must complete at their institution, increasing tuition revenue. Similarly, community colleges often lack the resources to provide adequate advising and transfer support, leaving students without the guidance needed to navigate these challenges effectively.

These systemic issues create ripple effects that harm not only individual students but also the broader economy. Delayed degree completion reduces students' lifetime earning potential, while higher debt levels constrain their financial freedom. Additionally, the inefficiencies of the transfer process contribute to lower bachelor's degree attainment rates, limiting the pool of skilled workers needed for high-demand industries.

To address these issues, higher education systems must prioritize streamlining transfer pathways. Comprehensive articulation agreements that clearly map out transferable credits and degree requirements are essential. Shared advising systems that involve both community colleges and universities can provide students with consistent guidance, ensuring that they make informed decisions about their coursework and transfer plans. States like Florida and California, which have implemented robust transfer frameworks, offer models for how collaboration can reduce credit loss, lower costs, and improve student outcomes (Bailey et al., 2015).

By breaking down the barriers within the transfer process, colleges and universities can fulfill their shared mission of expanding access to higher education and promoting student success. Addressing the transfer bottleneck is not only a matter of efficiency but also one of equity, ensuring that students pursuing this pathway are not penalized for their choice to begin at a community college. Without meaningful reform, the divide between these two segments of higher education will continue to cost students precious time and money, undermining the promise of a more accessible and affordable higher education system.

Community Colleges AS and AAS Degrees in Skilled Trades

Community colleges have long positioned themselves as champions of accessible, affordable, and practical education. In recent years, they've expanded their offerings of Associate of Science (AS) and Associate of Applied Science (AAS) degrees in technical and skilled trades fields such as HVAC (Heating, Ventilation, and Air Conditioning), Automotive Technology, Welding, Electrical Technology, and more. While these programs claim to respond to industry demands and offer students clear pathways to well-paying careers, critics argue that they prioritize institutional revenue over student success.

HVAC Technology: A Misaligned Approach?

HVAC programs at community colleges often emphasize hands-on training in system installation, maintenance, and repair. They are designed to prepare students for certifications such as EPA Section 608 or NATE credentials. However, this training could be completed in as little as 8 to 10 weeks through specialized trade schools, rather than the AAS 2 year college degree.

By requiring general education courses like English, humanities, and social sciences, community colleges burden students with irrelevant coursework. These requirements inflate the time and cost of earning a degree while providing little added value for future HVAC technicians, whose careers depend more on practical skills and certifications than academic credentials.

Automotive Technology: Skills or a Degree?

AAS degrees in Automotive Technology equip students with technical knowledge to diagnose, repair, and maintain vehicles, including modern electric and hybrid systems. While community colleges tout partnerships with manufacturers like Toyota or Ford, short-term automotive training programs often provide the same skills in a fraction of the time and cost.

Instead of focusing solely on skills, community colleges require students to complete unrelated coursework, delaying their entry into the workforce and increasing their financial burden. This approach raises questions about whether the true goal is preparing students for careers or maximizing institutional revenue.

Welding Technology: Overcomplicating a Simple Path

Community college welding programs teach essential techniques such as TIG, MIG, and arc welding, alongside coursework in blueprint reading and metallurgy. While these programs may result in certifications from organizations like the American Welding Society

(AWS), students could achieve the same outcomes faster and cheaper through direct-to-career welding programs.

The additional time spent in general education courses not only extends program lengths but also diverts students from gaining immediate, practical experience. This model serves institutional interests by generating more tuition revenue rather than focusing on what's best for students.

The General Education Dilemma

Fields like plumbing, renewable energy installation, and industrial maintenance are similarly affected by the community college model. While these programs claim to align with industry needs, their structure often prioritizes degree completion over rapid workforce readiness.

The inclusion of general education requirements adds unnecessary time and expense to the educational journey, creating barriers for students who could otherwise enter the workforce quickly through trade-specific training programs.

Institutional Money Over Student Needs

At their core, AS and AAS degrees in skilled trades reflect a larger issue: the institutional focus on revenue generation. By requiring students to enroll in multi-year degree programs with general education requirements, community colleges secure more tuition dollars at the expense of students' time and financial well-being.

A Better Alternative: Direct-to-Career Training

Trade schools and industry-sponsored programs provide a faster, more cost-effective path to skilled careers. These programs eliminate irrelevant coursework and focus solely on the technical skills and certifications employers demand. For example:

- **HVAC Training**: Short-term programs lead directly to certifications like EPA Section 608, allowing students to enter the field in a few months.

- **Automotive Repair**: Manufacturer-specific programs provide cutting-edge training tailored to current industry needs.

- **Welding**: Intensive, hands-on courses prepare students for AWS certification and immediate employment.

These alternatives prioritize student success, ensuring graduates are workforce-ready without unnecessary delays or costs.

Empowering Students and Communities

While community colleges argue that their degree programs contribute to local economic stability, the reality is more complex. Students burdened with debt and extended timelines often face financial and emotional stress, undermining the very stability these programs claim to support.

Direct-to-career training programs, on the other hand, provide immediate benefits to both students and their communities. Graduates quickly enter high-demand fields, boosting local economies without the overhead of lengthy degree programs.

Reclaiming the Student-First Approach

Community colleges must fundamentally reevaluate their approach to technical and skilled trades education. By prioritizing institutional revenue through multi-year degree programs with unnecessary general education requirements, they risk turning what should be an affordable and efficient pathway into a financial and time-consuming trap.

Revenue-Based Funding: The Hidden Driver

Community colleges often operate under revenue-based funding models, where enrollment numbers and credit hours drive institutional income. This creates a perverse incentive to design programs that maximize the number of courses a student must take rather than focusing on their practical career needs.

For example, technical fields such as HVAC, welding, and automotive repair often require certifications and hands-on training—not an associate degree. Yet, many community colleges bundle these programs with unrelated coursework to inflate credit hours.

This practice disproportionately affects the populations community colleges are meant to serve—working adults, low-income students, and career changers. These students often juggle work, family responsibilities, and limited resources, making the added time and cost of irrelevant coursework an undue burden.

Rebuilding Trust and Fulfilling the Mission

Community colleges are uniquely positioned to address workforce needs while providing accessible education. However, this potential can only be realized if they prioritize students over revenue. By shifting to a student-first model focused on efficiency, affordability, and workforce alignment, community colleges can regain the trust of their communities and fulfill their mission of creating equitable opportunities.

Education should be a ladder to success, not a treadmill that leaves students exhausted and financially drained. The time for change is now—community colleges must evolve to meet the needs of their students, not their bottom lines.

The diverging purposes of community colleges, colleges, and universities highlight both the opportunities and challenges inherent in a diverse higher education system. Universities excel in driving innovation and creating new knowledge, colleges focus on broader academic pathways, and community colleges historically prioritized accessibility and workforce development to meet the immediate needs of students and their communities. However, this ideal model is increasingly overshadowed by an institutional machine focused on revenue generation, turning what should be a student-first system into one that primarily feeds the financial demands of the institution.

Community colleges, in particular, have drifted from their original mission of providing affordable, efficient, and accessible education. Instead of streamlining programs to equip students with the skills and certifications they need to succeed in the workforce quickly, these institutions often embed excessive general education requirements into multi-year programs. This unnecessarily prolongs students' educational journeys, driving up costs and diverting them from their ultimate career goals. The emphasis on maximizing enrollment numbers and credit hours reflects an institutional strategy to secure funding and revenue rather than serving students' best interests.

This systemic shift underscores a broken model—one that places institutional profit over practical training, equitable access, and student success. By forcing students into prolonged programs with irrelevant coursework, community colleges alienate the very populations they are meant to uplift: working adults, low-income individuals, and career changers seeking fast, affordable pathways to better livelihoods. The result is a cycle where students are saddled with debt, delayed workforce entry, and a diminished sense of trust in higher education.

Moreover, the systemic focus on prestige at universities, broad academic programming at colleges, and inflated degree requirements at community colleges undermines the promise of higher education as a collaborative ecosystem. Rather than harmonizing their unique strengths—universities as research hubs, colleges as academic bridges, and community colleges as workforce incubators—these institutions often operate in silos, driven by self-serving priorities.

To truly serve students and society, higher education must dismantle the revenue-first model and reimagine itself as a student-first system. This requires:

- **Streamlined pathways** that eliminate unnecessary coursework and focus on skills directly tied to career outcomes.

- **Transparency** about costs, timelines, and program outcomes to empower students to make informed decisions.

- **Collaborative alignment** among institutions to create seamless transitions for students across academic and career pathways.

By bridging these divides, aligning goals, and valuing all pathways to success—whether through research, academic growth, or workforce preparation—we can restore higher education's mission as a public good. An inclusive, adaptable, and genuinely student-centered system is not only possible but essential to meet the demands of an increasingly complex and evolving world.

The time to abandon the broken, revenue-focused machine is now. Education must once again become a ladder of opportunity rather than a treadmill of financial exploitation, ensuring that institutions work for students—not the other way around.

Chapter 8

Barriers to Access in Higher Education

In a nation that prides itself on equal opportunity, higher education remains one of the most powerful tools for upward mobility, yet it is rife with barriers that exclude many from its promise. While the rhetoric of meritocracy suggests that anyone with talent and determination can succeed, the reality is far more complex. Persistent inequalities in access to higher education, driven by socioeconomic disparities, racial inequities, and systemic biases, ensure that many individuals are left behind. These challenges are compounded by entrenched practices such as standardized testing, legacy admissions, and implicit favoritism that disproportionately benefit affluent, white communities while sidelining others. As higher education continues to serve as a gateway to economic and social advancement, the question remains: who is granted entry, and who is left on the outside looking in? This chapter delves into the structural mechanisms that sustain exclusion, explores their implications for equity and inclusion, and examines pathways to dismantle these barriers for a more just and accessible educational system.

The Persistent Inequality in Access to Higher Education

Access to higher education has long been positioned as a cornerstone of the American Dream, symbolizing the pathway to upward mobility and economic opportunity. It offers the potential for individuals to break cycles of poverty, gain financial independence, and secure a better future for themselves and their families. However, this promise remains elusive for many, particularly for students from historically underserved and marginalized communities. Persistent inequalities rooted in socioeconomic status (SES), race, ethnicity, and geographic location limit access to higher education, creating systemic barriers that are deeply entrenched and difficult to dismantle.

The Role of Socioeconomic Status in Access

Socioeconomic status (SES) is one of the most significant predictors of whether a student will pursue and complete higher education. Families with higher incomes often have the resources to invest in their children's education from an early age, providing access to high-quality K-12 schools, extracurricular activities, and advanced placement (AP) courses that strengthen college applications. In contrast, students from low-income households frequently attend underfunded schools with fewer resources, larger class sizes, and limited access to college preparatory programs (Reardon et al., 2019). These disparities hinder academic achievement and readiness, reducing the likelihood that these students will successfully transition to higher education.

The financial burden of college further exacerbates these inequalities. Tuition and fees at both public and private institutions have steadily risen over the past several decades, while financial aid programs have not kept pace with these increases. The maximum Pell Grant, a crucial financial aid resource for low-income students, covered approximately 77% of the cost of attending a four-year public institution in the 1980s. Today, it covers less than 30%, forcing many students to take on substantial debt or forgo college altogether (Baum et al., 2021). This economic barrier disproportionately affects low-income students, who are often forced to make decisions based on affordability rather than academic fit or long-term career aspirations.

Racial and Ethnic Disparities

Racial and ethnic disparities compound the challenges posed by socioeconomic inequality. Black, Hispanic, and Indigenous students are significantly underrepresented in higher education, particularly at selective colleges and universities. These disparities are rooted in systemic inequities that affect educational opportunities from early childhood onward. Schools in predominantly minority neighborhoods are more likely to be underfunded, lack experienced teachers, and offer fewer advanced courses compared to schools in predominantly white neighborhoods. This lack of access to quality education limits academic preparation and reduces college readiness among students of color (Reardon et al., 2019).

In addition to resource disparities, structural barriers such as discriminatory admissions practices and implicit bias further limit access. For example, many colleges place significant weight on standardized test scores in their admissions decisions, despite evidence that these scores are strongly correlated with family income and access to test preparation resources (Soares, 2012). Because students of color are more likely to come from low-income households, they are disproportionately disadvantaged by this emphasis on testing.

Even when students of color overcome these initial barriers and enroll in college, they often face additional challenges, including a lack of representation, limited access to mentors, and hostile campus climates. These factors contribute to lower retention and graduation rates among Black, Hispanic, and Indigenous students compared to their white peers (Nichols & Schak, 2020).

Geographic Inequalities

Geographic location is another critical factor influencing access to higher education. Rural and remote areas often lack proximity to colleges and universities, making it more difficult for students to pursue higher education without leaving their communities. Limited access to reliable transportation and broadband internet further exacerbates this challenge, particularly for students who rely on online courses or resources to supplement their education.

Additionally, cultural attitudes in rural areas may discourage higher education. Many rural students grow up in communities where attending college is not seen as a priority or necessity, particularly if local economies are centered on industries that do not require a degree. This cultural dynamic can create a sense of ambivalence or even resistance toward higher education, leading to lower enrollment rates among rural students (Johnson & Strange, 2005).

Intersectionality of Barriers

The intersection of these factors creates compounded disadvantages for many students. For instance, a low-income Black student living in a rural area may face financial barriers, racial discrimination, and geographic isolation simultaneously, significantly reducing their likelihood of accessing and completing higher education. Addressing these inequalities requires an intersectional approach that acknowledges and addresses the multiple dimensions of disadvantage that many students face.

Toward Equity in Access

Achieving equity in higher education access requires systemic change at both the institutional and policy levels. Institutions must actively address biases in admissions practices, increase financial aid, and invest in support programs for underserved students. Outreach initiatives that target underrepresented communities, such as partnerships with low-income schools and mentorship programs, can help build a pipeline to higher education.

At the policy level, federal and state governments must increase funding for public education, expand need-based financial aid, and implement programs to reduce the cost of attendance, such as free community college initiatives. Additionally, investments in minority-serving institutions and rural colleges can help bridge gaps in access and ensure that students from all backgrounds have the opportunity to pursue higher education.

Understanding and addressing these structural barriers is essential for creating an educational system that fulfills its promise as a pathway to opportunity and upward mobility. Only by confronting the deep-seated inequalities in access to higher education can we move closer to a society where everyone, regardless of their background, has a fair chance to succeed.

Chapter 9

Systemic Bias in College Admissions

Collage admissions process is often portrayed as a meritocratic system that rewards talent and hard work, yet it is riddled with practices that perpetuate inequality and privilege. Standardized testing, legacy admissions, and systemic bias operate as significant gatekeepers, disproportionately benefiting affluent, white students while marginalizing underrepresented and low-income applicants. These entrenched mechanisms, often justified as measures of merit or tradition, reinforce structural inequities and hinder efforts to create a truly inclusive and equitable higher education system. Understanding their role is crucial to dismantling barriers that limit access and opportunity for those who need it most.

Standardized Testing

Standardized testing has served as a cornerstone of the college admissions process in the United States for decades. Proponents argue that tests such as the SAT and ACT offer an objective, uniform measure of academic ability, ostensibly enabling colleges to identify talented students regardless of their backgrounds. This rationale is rooted in the belief that standardized tests provide a common yardstick by which all applicants can be evaluated, allowing colleges to compare students from vastly different schools and curricula. However, mounting evidence suggests that these tests are far from equitable and, in practice, often serve to reinforce existing disparities in educational opportunity and outcomes.

The Link Between Test Scores and Socioeconomic Status

A significant body of research demonstrates a strong correlation between standardized test scores and family income, with wealthier students consistently outperforming their lower-income peers (Soares, 2012). This disparity arises not from inherent differences in ability, but from unequal access to resources that give wealthier students a substantial advantage. High-income families can afford private tutoring, test preparation courses, and study materials that are out of reach for many low-income families. Additionally, affluent students are more likely to attend schools that offer SAT or ACT preparation as part of the curriculum, further enhancing their performance on these exams.

The ability to take standardized tests multiple times is another factor that advantages wealthier students. Data from the College Board reveals that students who retake the SAT frequently see significant score improvements. However, the cost of registration and additional testing sessions can be prohibitive for low-income students, effectively limiting their chances to improve their scores. This disparity underscores how standardized tests, far from leveling the playing field, often magnify existing inequalities.

Cultural Bias in Standardized Tests

Beyond socioeconomic factors, standardized tests have also been criticized for cultural bias. Test questions and formats often reflect the experiences and knowledge of middle- and upper-class white students, while marginalizing those from diverse cultural backgrounds. For example, vocabulary and reading comprehension sections may include references that are more familiar to students from affluent, English-speaking households, disadvantaging students whose first language is not English or who come from underrepresented communities. Such biases call into question the validity of these tests as measures of academic ability and potential.

The Shift to Test-Optional Policies

The COVID-19 pandemic prompted many colleges and universities to adopt test-optional admissions policies, raising important questions about the future of standardized testing. These policies were initially implemented in response to logistical challenges posed by the pandemic, such as widespread test cancellations. However, their adoption has continued beyond the immediate crisis, with some institutions permanently eliminating test requirements.

Research suggests that test-optional policies can increase applications from underrepresented groups, including low-income students and students of color, by removing a significant barrier to entry (Hiss & Franks, 2014). For these students, standardized testing often represents an insurmountable hurdle due to financial constraints or limited access to preparation resources. By making these tests optional, colleges can encourage a broader and more diverse applicant pool.

However, critics argue that test-optional policies do not address deeper inequities in the admissions process. Even without test scores, affluent students can still leverage other advantages, such as access to polished application essays, extracurricular activities, and private college admissions counselors. These elements, like standardized testing, reflect broader disparities in resources and opportunities, allowing wealthier students to maintain their competitive edge.

The Future of Standardized Testing

The shift to test-optional admissions has sparked a broader conversation about the role of standardized testing in college admissions. Advocates for test elimination argue that these exams are outdated and exclusionary, failing to capture the full range of talents and abilities that students bring to the table. They contend that alternative metrics, such as high school GPA, can provide a more accurate and equitable measure of student potential. High school GPA is consistently shown to be a stronger predictor of college success than standardized test scores, as it reflects sustained effort and achievement over time rather than performance on a single test.

On the other hand, some educators and institutions continue to defend standardized testing as a valuable tool for identifying academically talented students, particularly those from underresourced schools. Without standardized tests, they argue, admissions officers may lack a common benchmark for evaluating applicants from disparate educational backgrounds. This perspective highlights the need for holistic admissions practices that consider multiple aspects of a student's profile, from academic performance to extracurricular involvement and personal challenges.

Legacy Admissions

Legacy admissions represent one of the most contentious practices in higher education, perpetuating privilege and inequality while raising significant ethical and practical concerns. Under this policy, applicants with familial ties to alumni are given preferential treatment during the admissions process, often receiving a substantial boost in their chances of acceptance. While legacy admissions have long been a tradition at elite institutions, they have increasingly come under scrutiny for reinforcing systemic inequities and undermining the meritocratic ideals of higher education.

The Advantages of Legacy Applicants

Legacy applicants enjoy a significant advantage in the admissions process. A study by Hurwitz (2011) revealed that legacy applicants are three times more likely to gain admission to elite colleges and universities than non-legacy applicants with comparable academic qualifications. This preferential treatment applies not only to direct descendants, such as children of alumni, but also in some cases to extended family members. The practice disproportionately benefits white, affluent families, as these groups have historically been the primary beneficiaries of access to elite institutions.

The roots of legacy admissions can be traced back to the early 20th century, when they were introduced as a means to preserve the influence of wealthy, predominantly white families and exclude growing numbers of immigrant and minority applicants. Although the overtly discriminatory intent of these policies has since diminished, their impact continues to reinforce systemic inequities. For example, because historically marginalized groups have only recently gained broader access to elite institutions, they are underrepresented among alumni networks. Consequently, their descendants are less likely to benefit from legacy preferences.

Financial Incentives vs. Social Responsibility

Advocates of legacy admissions often argue that these policies bolster alumni engagement and encourage philanthropic contributions. While legacy students may bring financial benefits to institutions, this justification comes at the cost of social responsibility. Colleges and universities, particularly those receiving public funding, have a moral obligation to ensure that their admissions processes promote equity and inclusivity. Legacy admissions stand in direct opposition to these principles, prioritizing privilege over potential and merit.

Calls for Reform

Growing criticism of legacy admissions has sparked calls for reform. Several prominent institutions, including Johns Hopkins University and Amherst College, have recently eliminated legacy preferences in an effort to promote equity and level the playing field. These decisions reflect a broader shift in higher education toward reexamining long-standing practices that perpetuate inequality. However, widespread change remains slow, as many elite institutions continue to cling to legacy admissions, citing financial and cultural reasons.

Holistic Admissions: A Step Toward Equity

To address systemic bias in college admissions, institutions must adopt more holistic approaches that consider a wide range of factors beyond test scores and legacy status. Holistic admissions evaluate applicants based on their unique circumstances, including personal achievements, life challenges, and contributions to their communities. This approach recognizes the diverse pathways through which students demonstrate potential and aims to create a more inclusive and representative student body.

The Need for Accountability and Transparency

Transparency and accountability are crucial to dismantling bias in college admissions. Institutions must provide clear and accessible data on their admissions processes, including the use of standardized tests, legacy preferences, and other criteria. Such transparency allows for greater scrutiny and ensures that colleges are held accountable for their commitment to equity and inclusion.

The systemic biases embedded in college admissions undermine the promise of higher education as a pathway to opportunity and social mobility. Standardized testing and legacy admissions are not merely relics of tradition; they are active mechanisms of exclusion that perpetuate privilege and inequity. By critically examining these practices and embracing reform, colleges and universities can take meaningful steps toward creating a more equitable and inclusive system. It is only through collective action and sustained advocacy that we can break down the gatekeepers and ensure that higher education serves as a true engine of opportunity for all.

Chapter 10

The Overemphasis on College Degrees

The growing emphasis on college degrees as the ultimate measure of success has profoundly shaped educational priorities, workforce expectations, and societal values. While higher education has long been celebrated as a gateway to opportunity, the singular focus on a four-year degree has marginalized other equally valuable pathways, such as vocational training and certifications. This "college-for-all" mindset not only undermines the importance of diverse educational routes but also contributes to systemic issues like credential inflation, labor market inefficiencies, and widening inequalities. For those without degrees, the consequences are particularly severe, as rigid educational requirements often exclude them from meaningful employment opportunities. This chapter explores the overemphasis on college degrees, examining how it devalues vocational education, perpetuates credential inflation, and limits the prospects of non-degree holders, while proposing more inclusive approaches to education and workforce development.

College-for-All Mindset Undermines Vocational Training

The "college-for-all" mindset, which has shaped American educational policy and cultural attitudes for decades, posits that a four-year college degree is the ultimate pathway to economic mobility and personal success. While this narrative has been instrumental in increasing college attendance rates, it has also sidelined alternative educational pathways, particularly vocational and technical training. This singular focus has created a false dichotomy in which students are often led to believe that college is the only worthwhile option, undermining the value of vocational education and contributing to significant labor market imbalances.

Vocational training encompasses programs designed to prepare individuals for specific trades or industries, including manufacturing, healthcare, information technology, construction, and skilled trades such as plumbing and electrical work. These programs provide practical, hands-on experience and are often aligned with current labor market needs, enabling students to transition seamlessly into well-paying jobs. For example, according to the Bureau of Labor Statistics, many skilled trades offer median annual wages comparable to or exceeding those of bachelor's degree holders, often without the burden of student loan debt.

Despite these benefits, vocational training is frequently stigmatized as a less prestigious or "second-choice" option, reserved for students who are perceived as less academically capable. This stigma stems from deep-seated cultural biases that equate success with white-collar professions and view blue-collar work as less desirable. The result is a persistent undervaluation of vocational education, which not only discourages students from pursuing these pathways but also exacerbates shortages in essential skilled labor fields (Symonds et al., 2011).

Moreover, the emphasis on college degrees has led to systemic underinvestment in career and technical education (CTE) programs at the high school and community college levels. Federal funding for CTE programs has remained stagnant or declined in real terms over the past two decades, leaving many schools unable to provide the state-of-the-art facilities, equipment, and qualified instructors needed to deliver high-quality training (Advance CTE, 2020). In contrast, substantial resources continue to flow toward college preparatory programs, further reinforcing the notion that a four-year degree is the only legitimate path to success.

This mindset also fails to account for the realities of the modern labor market. Many industries face significant shortages of middle-skill workers—those with more than a high school diploma but less than a bachelor's degree. These jobs, which include roles such as HVAC technicians, dental hygienists, and IT support specialists, are essential to the economy and offer stable, well-paying careers. By promoting the college-for-all narrative at the expense of vocational training, the education system risks both leaving critical jobs unfilled and denying students the opportunity to pursue fulfilling and lucrative careers that align with their skills and interests.

Efforts to address this imbalance must focus on destigmatizing vocational education and integrating it more fully into the broader education system. Public awareness campaigns highlighting the value of skilled trades, increased funding for CTE programs, and partnerships between schools and industries to create apprenticeship opportunities are critical steps toward ensuring that all students have access to pathways that meet their unique talents and aspirations.

Complete College America and Other Programs

Programs like Complete College America (CCA) have emerged as central players in advancing the college-for-all agenda. Founded in 2009, CCA seeks to increase college completion rates by promoting policies and strategies that help students earn their degrees more efficiently. Its initiatives include guided pathways, performance-based funding models, co-requisite remediation, and the use of data analytics to track student progress (Complete College America, 2023). While these strategies have achieved measurable success in boosting completion rates, they also reinforce the overemphasis on four-year degrees, potentially marginalizing other forms of postsecondary education.

One of CCA's key initiatives, the guided pathways model, aims to streamline the college experience by providing students with clear, structured degree plans that reduce time to completion and minimize unnecessary course-taking. While this approach helps students navigate the complexities of higher education, it may inadvertently narrow their focus to traditional degree programs, overlooking alternative credentials such as certifications and technical training. These alternatives, while equally valuable in the workforce, often lack the visibility and institutional support needed to thrive under such models.

Similarly, performance-based funding, another pillar of CCA's strategy, ties state funding for colleges and universities to metrics such as graduation rates and job placement outcomes. While this model incentivizes institutions to prioritize student success, it can also create pressure to prioritize traditional degree programs over non-degree pathways. Institutions may be less inclined to invest in vocational and technical programs if these are not explicitly rewarded under performance-based funding frameworks.

Other initiatives, such as America's College Promise, have sought to expand access to higher education by promoting tuition-free community college programs. These policies represent a significant step toward reducing financial barriers for low-income students, yet they often emphasize transfer pathways to four-year institutions rather than direct-entry vocational training. Without complementary efforts to strengthen CTE programs and apprenticeships, such initiatives risk perpetuating the college-for-all narrative at the expense of alternative educational pathways.

To ensure that these programs support all students equitably, policymakers and educators must broaden their definitions of success in higher education. This includes recognizing the value of non-degree credentials, integrating vocational training into broader completion agendas, and aligning funding models with the diverse needs of the labor market.

Devaluation of Degrees and Credential Inflation Phenomenon

The rapid expansion of college access over the past several decades has led to a dramatic increase in the number of degree holders in the workforce. While this trend reflects progress in making higher education more accessible, it has also contributed to the devaluation of degrees and the phenomenon of credential inflation. Credential inflation occurs when the educational requirements for jobs rise unnecessarily, often without corresponding increases in the skills needed to perform those jobs (Collins, 2019).

This phenomenon has several far-reaching consequences. First, it places an undue financial burden on students, who must invest more time and money into obtaining credentials that may not guarantee better job prospects or higher wages. Between 2010 and 2020, the average cost of attendance at public four-year universities rose by 31%, forcing many students to take on substantial debt to earn degrees that are increasingly required for entry-level positions (College Board, 2021). This financial strain is especially acute for low-income students, who are more likely to rely on loans and may face higher default rates if their post-graduation earnings fail to meet expectations.

Second, credential inflation exacerbates social and economic inequality. Non-degree holders, who are disproportionately from low-income and minority backgrounds, are often excluded from jobs for which they are otherwise qualified simply because they lack the "right" credential. This exclusion creates a barrier to upward mobility, perpetuating cycles of poverty and inequality.

Finally, credential inflation creates inefficiencies in the labor market. Employers may struggle to fill positions because they require unnecessary degrees, while qualified candidates are overlooked. For example, a 2017 report by Burning Glass Technologies found that employers often require bachelor's degrees for jobs that historically did not require them, such as administrative assistants and manufacturing supervisors. This mismatch between job requirements and workforce skills contributes to labor shortages in critical industries and inflates hiring costs for employers.

Addressing credential inflation requires a cultural shift away from equating success with degree attainment. Employers can play a key role by adopting skills-based hiring practices that prioritize relevant experience and competencies over formal credentials. Policymakers should also incentivize alternative pathways, such as apprenticeships and certifications, that provide students with the skills needed to succeed without the financial burden of a four-year degree.

The Consequences for Non-Degree Holders in the Job Market

The overemphasis on college degrees has profound implications for non-degree holders, who often face significant barriers to entry in the job market. Despite possessing skills and experience that make them well-suited for many roles, these individuals are frequently excluded from consideration due to rigid educational requirements. This phenomenon, sometimes referred to as "degree discrimination," reinforces socioeconomic inequality and limits opportunities for upward mobility.

Non-degree holders are more likely to be employed in low-wage jobs with limited benefits and few opportunities for advancement. According to the Georgetown Center on Education and the Workforce, individuals with only a high school diploma earn, on average, $1 million less over their lifetime than those with a bachelor's degree (Carnevale et al., 2021). This income disparity reflects not only the higher wages associated with degree-requiring jobs but also the limited career progression available to non-degree holders.

The focus on degrees also undervalues alternative credentials, such as industry certifications and vocational training. These pathways often provide individuals with the skills needed to excel in high-demand industries, yet they lack the same recognition as traditional degrees. Employers may overlook candidates with certifications in favor of degree holders, even when the former possess more relevant skills and experience. This disconnect highlights the need for greater recognition of non-degree credentials in hiring practices.

Efforts to address these challenges must include a shift toward more inclusive hiring practices and expanded access to alternative education and training programs. Employers can adopt skills-based hiring models that evaluate candidates based on their abilities rather than their formal education. Additionally, workforce development initiatives should prioritize accessible, high-quality training programs for non-degree holders, ensuring that all individuals have opportunities to succeed in the modern economy.

Degree Inflation and Misaligned Educational Models

Higher education in the United States has long been viewed as a pathway to success, yet many degrees have questionable value in the job market. Fields like Social Sciences, Humanities, Fine Arts, and General Liberal Arts sedges (i.e. sociology, philosophy, human geography, art history, art, communications, and more) while fostering critical thinking and analytical skills, often fail to align with workforce demands. Graduates with these degrees frequently struggle to find well-paying jobs in their fields, leading to underemployment and significant student debt. Although these disciplines contribute to intellectual and cultural development, they do not necessarily translate into tangible career outcomes for many students. This disconnect raises concerns about whether the substantial financial investment required for these degrees is justified, particularly when many graduates find themselves navigating a saturated job market with limited opportunities (Vedder et al., 2013). The persistent narrative that any degree guarantees success misleads students, contributing to the broader issue of degree inflation.

Compounding this issue is the structure of professional degrees in the U.S., particularly in medicine. Unlike countries such as the United Kingdom or Australia, where students can enter medical school directly after high school and complete their training in five to six years, aspiring physicians in the United States must first earn a four-year bachelor's degree before entering medical school. This requirement not only adds to the financial burden but also extends the time to career entry unnecessarily. A more efficient model would streamline the process, transitioning to a five-year MD program where the first year includes foundational premedical coursework. Such a reform would align the U.S. with global best practices and reduce the barriers that discourage many capable students from pursuing medical careers (Mullan et al., 2010).

This degree inflation and misalignment of educational models have led to broader systemic issues. The emphasis on college degrees for all has flooded the labor market with graduates holding qualifications that neither equip them with job-ready skills nor meet current workforce demands. This phenomenon, known as credential creep, pushes employers to raise educational requirements for entry-level positions, perpetuating the cycle of degree inflation. As a result, higher education becomes less efficient and more expensive, leaving many students with degrees that do not deliver the expected return on investment (Carnevale et al., 2010).

Reforming these models is critical to restoring the value of higher education. Colleges and universities must prioritize workforce-driven education by offering degrees and certifications tied to industry needs. For example, compressing professional programs like the United States MD, DDS, DMD, DO, DVM, OD, DC, DNP, and other non-academic degree programs into shorter, more focused tracks would not only reduce costs but also improve accessibility for aspiring professionals. Additionally, expanding trade school programs and community college pathways can provide students with viable alternatives to traditional degrees, fostering career readiness without the burden of excessive debt. By addressing these inefficiencies and misalignments, higher education can better serve students and the broader society, ensuring that degrees have both intellectual and economic value.

The overemphasis on college degrees has created a system that undervalues alternative educational pathways, exacerbates credential inflation, and deepens inequalities in the job market. While higher education remains a powerful tool for personal and professional advancement, it is not the only route to success, nor should it be treated as such. The problem with degree inflation and misaligned educational models is emblematic of this systemic issue, as it has led to inefficiencies in both education and workforce development. Degrees in fields with limited career applicability and unnecessarily prolonged professional programs highlight the need for a reevaluation of how education serves societal and economic needs.

Vocational training, certifications, and skills-based education are vital components of a robust and inclusive workforce, offering opportunities that align with the needs of the economy and the diverse aspirations of individuals. By streamlining degree programs, addressing credential inflation, and destigmatizing vocational education, we can foster a system that prioritizes efficiency and equity.

To move forward, we must challenge the "college-for-all" narrative, reimagine educational priorities, and foster a culture that respects and invests in all pathways to success. By embracing a broader definition of education and rethinking rigid hiring practices, we can create a system that values skills, reduces barriers, and ensures that all individuals—whether pursuing a degree, certification, or hands-on training—have the opportunity to thrive.

Chapter 11

Decline of Intellectual Freedom and Debate

The ability to freely exchange ideas and engage in rigorous debate has long been a cornerstone of higher education, fostering intellectual growth, innovation, and societal progress. However, in recent years, this foundational principle has come under threat, as ideological biases, the rise of "safe spaces," and increasing political polarization have reshaped the academic landscape. These changes have sparked a broader conversation about the balance between inclusivity and free speech, the role of ideological diversity in education, and the impact of these trends on critical thinking skills. This chapter explores how the decline of intellectual freedom and open debate in higher education affects students, faculty, and the broader mission of academia, and it examines the consequences of a culture increasingly wary of dissent and ideological diversity.

The Liberal Agenda in Education Leading to Liberal Ideas Being Taught

The dominance of liberal ideologies within educational institutions has become a focal point of debate, with critics arguing that higher education increasingly functions as a conduit for progressive ideas. This perceived ideological imbalance has sparked concerns about the lack of representation for conservative or alternative viewpoints, raising questions about the role of academia in fostering diverse perspectives.

Studies consistently show that faculty members in higher education lean heavily to the political left. For example, the Higher Education Research Institute (HERI) reported in 2018 that nearly 60% of college professors identified as liberal, compared to just 12% who identified as conservative (HERI, 2018). This disparity is particularly pronounced in the humanities and social sciences, where curricula often focus on themes such as social justice, systemic inequities, and environmental sustainability. While these topics are important, critics argue that the framing and delivery of such content often reflect a progressive lens, limiting the exploration of competing ideas.

The predominance of liberal ideologies is sometimes justified as a natural alignment between academic values—such as inclusivity, equity, and critical inquiry—and progressive principles. However, this alignment can create a feedback loop in which liberal perspectives dominate faculty hiring, curriculum development, and campus culture. For instance, when hiring committees prioritize candidates whose research aligns with progressive paradigms, alternative viewpoints may be excluded, reducing ideological diversity within departments.

This imbalance has real consequences for students. Research shows that exposure to diverse perspectives is crucial for developing critical thinking skills and intellectual resilience. When academic environments primarily promote liberal ideas, students may miss opportunities to challenge their assumptions and engage with contrasting viewpoints. This dynamic risks creating intellectual echo chambers, where prevailing ideologies are rarely questioned, and dissenting opinions are marginalized.

Efforts to address this imbalance have included inviting conservative speakers to campuses, hosting debates on contentious topics, and integrating diverse perspectives into coursework. However, these initiatives often face resistance from vocal segments of campus communities, who may view opposing ideologies as harmful or incompatible with institutional values. The challenge for higher education is to balance the promotion of inclusivity and equity with the need to foster robust intellectual debate.

The Rise of "Safe Spaces" and the Chilling Effect on Free Speech

The emergence of "safe spaces" on college campuses has sparked a heated debate about the balance between creating inclusive environments and preserving free speech. Originally intended as supportive spaces for marginalized students to discuss their experiences and find community, safe spaces have expanded in scope and purpose over the years. While proponents see them as essential for fostering equity, critics argue that they have evolved into tools for suppressing dissent and shielding students from uncomfortable ideas.

Supporters of safe spaces emphasize their role in addressing systemic inequities and ensuring that students from underrepresented groups feel valued and respected. For example, LGBTQ+ students, racial minorities, and individuals who have experienced trauma often rely on safe spaces as environments where they can express themselves without fear of judgment or hostility. Research highlights that such spaces can improve mental health outcomes and academic performance for marginalized students, enabling them to thrive in settings where they might otherwise feel excluded (Clark, 2018).

However, critics argue that the expansion of safe spaces has led to unintended consequences, including the stifling of open dialogue. In some cases, students and faculty report feeling hesitant to express unpopular or controversial opinions for fear of backlash or being labeled as insensitive. This phenomenon, known as the "chilling effect," discourages individuals from participating in debates or challenging prevailing norms, undermining the foundational purpose of higher education as a marketplace of ideas.

The chilling effect is exacerbated by instances in which invited speakers are disinvited or events are canceled due to protests or administrative concerns. A 2019 survey by the Knight Foundation found that 68% of college students believed the climate on their campus discouraged them from expressing ideas that might offend others (Knight Foundation, 2019). This self-censorship undermines intellectual freedom, as students and faculty become reluctant to explore controversial topics or advocate for minority viewpoints.

Balancing the need for safe spaces with the imperative of free speech is a complex challenge. Institutions must ensure that safe spaces do not become echo chambers that exclude dissenting voices. Instead, they should be complemented by initiatives that promote open dialogue and equip students with the skills to engage constructively with diverse perspectives.

Political Polarization Within Academic Environments

The political polarization observed in society at large has found a potent expression within academic environments, creating a climate of division and mistrust. On college campuses, this polarization is often reflected in tensions between students, faculty, and administrators who hold differing ideological beliefs. These divisions can undermine the collaborative spirit necessary for intellectual growth and debate.

One manifestation of polarization is the rise of ideological echo chambers, in which individuals are primarily exposed to viewpoints that align with their own beliefs. This dynamic is particularly evident in fields such as sociology, anthropology, and gender studies, where dominant theoretical frameworks often align with progressive ideologies. While these frameworks contribute valuable insights, their prevalence can create an environment where alternative perspectives are dismissed or ignored.

Polarization also influences campus policies, such as those governing speech codes, diversity initiatives, and curriculum requirements. For instance, debates over mandatory courses on diversity or social justice often become battlegrounds for broader ideological conflicts. Progressives may view such courses as essential for promoting equity and understanding, while conservatives may see them as tools of indoctrination.

The impact of polarization extends beyond academic policies to campus culture, where political divisions can create an atmosphere of hostility. Conservative students frequently report feeling ostracized or marginalized, while liberal students may perceive conservative viewpoints as threats to their safety or values (Inbar & Lammers, 2012). These dynamics hinder the ability of campuses to serve as inclusive spaces for dialogue and mutual understanding.

Efforts to mitigate polarization include initiatives such as facilitated dialogues, intergroup workshops, and the promotion of bipartisan student organizations. These programs aim to bridge divides and foster a culture of respect and collaboration. However, their success often depends on the willingness of all parties to engage in good faith and prioritize shared goals over ideological purity.

The Impact on Intellectual Diversity and Critical Thinking Skills

The decline of intellectual freedom and debate on college campuses has profound implications for intellectual diversity and the development of critical thinking skills. Intellectual diversity—the inclusion of a wide range of perspectives, ideologies, and methodologies—is essential for fostering creativity, innovation, and robust academic inquiry. However, when certain viewpoints are marginalized or excluded, students are deprived of opportunities to engage with complex and often challenging ideas.

The suppression of dissenting perspectives contributes to a culture of intellectual conformity, where students feel pressure to align with dominant ideologies to succeed academically or socially. This conformity stifles creativity and limits the scope of critical inquiry, as students are less likely to question prevailing assumptions or explore unconventional approaches to problem-solving.

Moreover, the lack of exposure to diverse viewpoints undermines students' ability to evaluate arguments, assess evidence, and articulate their own positions. A robust academic environment should encourage students to grapple with difficult questions, confront their biases, and refine their beliefs through rigorous debate and reflection. Yet, the current climate of polarization and self-censorship often reduces complex issues to simplistic narratives, depriving students of the intellectual growth that comes from engaging with nuance and complexity.

To address these challenges, institutions must prioritize initiatives that promote intellectual humility, encourage open dialogue, and foster a culture of mutual respect. Faculty can play a crucial role by modeling constructive engagement with opposing views and integrating diverse perspectives into their teaching and research. Additionally, institutions should create policies that protect free speech while promoting inclusivity, ensuring that all members of the academic community feel empowered to share their ideas.

The decline of intellectual freedom and open debate in higher education poses significant challenges to the core mission of academia: fostering critical thinking, innovation, and a robust exchange of ideas. While efforts to promote inclusivity and protect vulnerable communities are vital, they must not come at the expense of intellectual diversity and free speech. A balanced approach is essential—one that supports respectful dialogue, encourages engagement with diverse perspectives, and equips students to navigate complex, often contentious ideas. By recommitting to these principles, higher education can reclaim its role as a crucible for critical inquiry and a space where all ideas are given the opportunity to be rigorously examined, debated, and understood. Only then can we prepare future generations to engage thoughtfully and constructively in an increasingly polarized world.

Chapter 12

Mental Health Crisis on Campus

Todays mental health crisis on college campuses has emerged as one of the most pressing challenges in higher education, reflecting the immense pressures faced by students in today's fast-paced and competitive world. Anxiety, depression, and other psychological disorders have reached record levels, fueled by academic demands, financial stress, and the lingering effects of social isolation exacerbated by the COVID-19 pandemic. While awareness of this crisis has grown, many colleges and universities remain ill-equipped to address the complex and evolving needs of their student populations. This chapter examines the multifaceted nature of the campus mental health crisis, exploring the growing prevalence of psychological challenges, the inadequacies of institutional support systems, and the interconnected impact of academic and financial pressures on student well-being.

The Growing Mental Health Challenges Faced by Students

The mental health crisis among college students has emerged as one of the defining challenges of modern higher education, with a staggering number of young adults reporting severe psychological struggles. Over the past two decades, this trend has intensified, placing unprecedented strain on students, faculty, and the limited support systems available on campuses. Anxiety, depression, and stress-related disorders have become the most frequently reported mental health issues, with nearly half of college students experiencing moderate to severe psychological distress, according to the American College Health Association (ACHA, 2021).

Increasing Prevalence of Mental Health Issues

Data from multiple studies underscores the scope of the problem. For example, the National College Health Assessment revealed that 63% of students reported feeling overwhelming anxiety during the past year, while 53% reported feelings of hopelessness, and 40% reported symptoms consistent with depression (ACHA, 2021). Suicide, one of the leading causes of death among young adults, has also seen a troubling rise, with nearly 14% of students reporting seriously considering suicide (Eisenberg et al., 2019). These statistics paint a grim picture of the mental health landscape on college campuses, signaling an urgent need for action.

Contributing Factors

Several factors are driving this mental health crisis, ranging from societal changes to specific stressors tied to the college experience:

1. Transition to College Life: The transition to college marks a significant life change for many students, often characterized by separation from familial support systems, the need to form new social networks, and increased personal and academic responsibilities. For first-year students in particular, these challenges can create feelings of isolation and uncertainty, increasing their vulnerability to anxiety and depression.

2. Academic Pressures: The competitive nature of higher education, coupled with the high expectations placed on students, creates an environment of relentless stress. Balancing demanding coursework, maintaining high grades, and preparing for post-graduation opportunities often lead to chronic stress and burnout.

3. Social Media and Technology: The rise of social media has added a new dimension to student mental health challenges. While platforms like Instagram and TikTok can foster connection, they also amplify feelings of inadequacy, loneliness, and fear of missing out (FOMO). A 2018 study by Twenge and Campbell found that heavy social media use correlates strongly with higher levels of anxiety and depression among young adults.

4. Global Events and Uncertainty: Recent global crises, such as the COVID-19 pandemic, have further exacerbated mental health issues. Prolonged periods of isolation, uncertainty about the future, and disruption to normal routines created a perfect storm of psychological challenges for many students. Financial pressures stemming from the pandemic also added to the burden, with many students or their families facing unemployment or reduced income.

Disproportionate Impacts on Marginalized Groups

The mental health crisis does not affect all students equally. Certain populations, including LGBTQ+ students, students of color, and first-generation college attendees, face unique stressors that compound the challenges of college life:

- LGBTQ+ Students: These students often experience higher levels of discrimination, rejection, and social isolation, leading to significantly elevated rates of anxiety, depression, and suicidal ideation compared to their heterosexual and cisgender peers (Trevor Project, 2020).

- Students of Color: For students from underrepresented racial and ethnic backgrounds, systemic inequities, microaggressions, and a lack of representation in faculty and administrative roles can contribute to feelings of alienation and exclusion, further exacerbating mental health challenges.

- First-Generation Students: Navigating the complexities of higher education without familial guidance creates additional pressure for first-generation students. These individuals often face heightened financial stress and a lack of academic and emotional support, leading to feelings of inadequacy and heightened vulnerability to mental health struggles.

Long-Term Implications

The long-term implications of untreated mental health issues among college students are profound. Academic performance often suffers, as symptoms such as difficulty concentrating, fatigue, and diminished motivation can lead to declining grades or withdrawal from courses. According to the Healthy Minds Network, students with untreated mental health conditions are twice as likely to leave college before completing their degree compared to their peers (Eisenberg et al., 2019). This dropout rate not only affects individual futures but also impacts institutional retention metrics and contributes to a broader societal loss of potential.

Moreover, untreated mental health issues can have lasting effects on students' personal and professional lives. Graduates who carry unresolved psychological challenges into the workforce may struggle with productivity, job retention, and interpersonal relationships, perpetuating cycles of distress and instability.

Addressing the growing mental health challenges faced by students requires a multifaceted approach. Institutions must expand access to counseling and support services, promote mental health literacy to reduce stigma, and implement policies that prioritize student well-being. By acknowledging the pervasive nature of this crisis and committing to systemic change, colleges and universities can help students navigate the complexities of higher education while fostering resilience and long-term mental health.

Factors Driving the Crisis

Several factors contribute to this mental health epidemic. Transitioning to college often presents a significant adjustment period, as students leave behind familiar support systems, navigate academic and social pressures, and face the reality of managing their own responsibilities. For many, this adjustment is compounded by feelings of loneliness, imposter syndrome, and fear of failure, which can escalate into chronic stress or depression if left unaddressed.

The COVID-19 pandemic has further intensified these struggles. Prolonged periods of isolation, remote learning, and uncertainty about the future created a perfect storm of psychological challenges for students. The National College Health Assessment (NCHA) reported a significant increase in loneliness, social anxiety, and feelings of disconnection during the pandemic, with many students struggling to adapt to a lack of face-to-face interaction and the blurred boundaries between academic and personal spaces (NCHA, 2022).

The pervasive influence of social media has also reshaped the mental health landscape. Platforms like Instagram, TikTok, and Snapchat, while providing avenues for connection, have also contributed to unhealthy comparisons, cyberbullying, and unrealistic expectations of success and appearance. Research by Twenge and Campbell (2018) highlights a strong correlation between heavy social media use and increased rates of anxiety and depression among young adults, exacerbating feelings of inadequacy and low self-esteem.

These challenges disproportionately affect marginalized populations, including LGBTQ+ students, racial minorities, and first-generation college attendees. LGBTQ+ students often report higher levels of discrimination, isolation, and mental health struggles, while students from underrepresented racial groups face additional pressures related to cultural assimilation, microaggressions, and systemic inequities (Clark et al., 2020). First-generation students frequently experience unique stressors such as familial expectations, financial burdens, and a lack of guidance in navigating the complexities of college life.

Long-Term Implications

The long-term implications of untreated mental health issues among college students extend far beyond individual well-being, affecting academic performance, institutional retention rates, and broader societal outcomes. Students grappling with anxiety, depression, or other mental health challenges often struggle to meet the demands of higher education, resulting in lower grades, incomplete coursework, and an increased likelihood of withdrawal. According to the Healthy Minds Study, students with untreated mental health conditions are twice as likely to leave college before completing their degree compared to their peers (Eisenberg et al., 2019). This heightened dropout rate underscores the urgent need for effective mental health interventions that support students throughout their academic journey.

The academic repercussions of untreated mental health conditions often create a domino effect. Dropping out of college can have significant consequences for students' career prospects, financial stability, and long-term quality of life. Without a degree, students face limited employment opportunities and reduced earning potential, perpetuating cycles of economic disadvantage. For first-generation and low-income students, these setbacks can be particularly devastating, as higher education is often seen as a pathway to breaking intergenerational poverty.

The ripple effects of untreated mental health issues also extend to institutions and society at large. Colleges and universities suffer financial losses when students drop out, as lower retention rates impact funding, rankings, and institutional reputation. Beyond the campus, society bears the cost of lost potential and productivity. The National Alliance on Mental Illness (NAMI) estimates that untreated mental health conditions cost the U.S. economy billions of dollars annually in lost productivity, increased healthcare expenses, and unemployment (NAMI, 2022).

The long-term consequences of untreated mental health conditions also affect personal relationships and community engagement.

Graduates who carry unresolved mental health struggles into adulthood may encounter difficulties forming and maintaining relationships, contributing to feelings of isolation and exacerbating their psychological challenges. These compounding effects highlight the critical need for colleges and universities to adopt a proactive, systemic approach to mental health care.

How Colleges Fail to Provide Adequate Support Systems

While the growing mental health crisis on campuses has garnered increased attention, many colleges and universities remain ill-equipped to provide the comprehensive care that students need. From understaffed counseling centers to systemic barriers that discourage help-seeking behavior, the existing infrastructure often fails to meet the rising demand for mental health services, leaving students without adequate support.

Inadequate Staffing and Resources

One of the most pressing issues is the chronic understaffing of campus counseling centers, which are often the primary resource for students seeking mental health support. The International Accreditation of Counseling Services recommends a ratio of one counselor per 1,000 students, yet most institutions fall short of this benchmark. A 2021 report by the Association for University and College Counseling Center Directors (AUCCCD) found that many institutions have ratios exceeding 1:2,000, with some even higher (Reetz et al., 2021). As a result, wait times for appointments often stretch to several weeks or even months, forcing students to delay or abandon their pursuit of care. These delays can be particularly harmful for students in crisis, who may experience worsening symptoms or feel discouraged from seeking help in the future.

Furthermore, many counseling centers operate on a short-term care model, which prioritizes brief interventions over ongoing therapy. While this model allows institutions to serve a larger number of students, it is often insufficient for addressing the needs of those with complex or chronic conditions. Students requiring specialized treatment for conditions such as post-traumatic stress disorder (PTSD), eating disorders, or substance abuse are frequently referred off-campus, where they encounter additional barriers. These barriers may include the high cost of treatment, limited availability of specialized providers, and logistical challenges such as transportation and insurance coverage. The reliance on external referrals underscores the gaps in campus-based care and highlights the systemic challenges of providing comprehensive mental health support.

Stigma and Cultural Barriers

Stigma remains a significant obstacle to mental health care, discouraging many students from seeking the support they need. Despite increasing public awareness and advocacy for mental health, societal attitudes still deter individuals from disclosing their struggles. This stigma is especially pronounced among male students, who often face cultural expectations to suppress vulnerability and "tough it out." Similarly, students from cultural or religious backgrounds where mental health is a taboo subject may feel pressured to avoid discussing their psychological challenges.

Research by Corrigan et al. (2014) found that fear of social repercussions is one of the most significant barriers to seeking mental health services. Students worry about being judged by peers, faculty, or even family members, leading them to internalize their struggles rather than seeking help. For LGBTQ+ students, stigma is often compounded by fears of discrimination or rejection, creating an additional layer of psychological stress.

Cultural and linguistic barriers also play a role in discouraging help-seeking behavior, particularly for students from immigrant or minority communities. These students may feel that campus counseling services are not equipped to understand or address their unique experiences, such as navigating racial discrimination, cultural identity conflicts, or intergenerational expectations. The lack of diverse representation among counseling staff can further alienate these students, reinforcing the perception that mental health services are not inclusive or accessible.

Systemic and Administrative Challenges

Administrative and financial constraints exacerbate the inadequacy of campus mental health services. Many colleges and universities face budgetary limitations that prevent them from hiring additional staff, expanding facilities, or implementing innovative programs. Mental health initiatives often compete with other institutional priorities, such as academic programs, infrastructure improvements, or athletics, for limited funding. In some cases, mental health is treated as a secondary concern, leaving institutions unprepared to address the scale of the crisis.

The absence of comprehensive mental health policies also contributes to fragmented care. Institutions without clear protocols for identifying and supporting students in distress may rely on reactive, case-by-case approaches that fail to address underlying systemic issues. For example, faculty and staff may lack training on how to recognize the signs of mental health struggles or how to connect students with appropriate resources. This lack of coordination creates gaps in care, leaving vulnerable students to navigate the complexities of mental health support on their own.

Innovative but Insufficient Solutions

In response to these challenges, some colleges have implemented innovative programs aimed at expanding access to mental health care. Peer support networks, telehealth services, and mental health awareness campaigns have emerged as promising strategies for reducing stigma and increasing the reach of counseling services. For example, peer-to-peer programs allow students to connect with trained peers who can provide emotional support and guidance, fostering a sense of community and reducing the stigma associated with seeking professional help.

Telehealth services have also gained popularity, particularly during the COVID-19 pandemic, as a way to provide more flexible and accessible care. Virtual counseling sessions enable students to receive support without the logistical challenges of traveling to an on-campus center. However, these solutions are often insufficient to address the full scope of the crisis. Peer support networks may lack the training to handle severe cases, while telehealth services require robust technological infrastructure and may not be suitable for all students.

Administrative and Financial Constraints

Budgetary and administrative constraints significantly limit the ability of colleges and universities to expand and improve their mental health services, creating systemic barriers that exacerbate the campus mental health crisis. Counseling centers often compete with other institutional priorities, such as infrastructure improvements, faculty hiring, and athletics programs, for limited funding. Mental health services are frequently underfunded relative to the scope and severity of the crisis, leaving them ill-equipped to meet the growing demand for care.

The lack of a clear institutional framework for addressing mental health challenges compounds these funding issues. Many colleges operate without comprehensive mental health policies, resulting in fragmented and reactive approaches that fail to address the underlying systemic causes of the crisis. For example, rather than investing in preventative programs that promote mental well-being, institutions often focus resources on responding to crises after they occur. This reactive approach places immense strain on counseling centers and fails to create an environment that fosters long-term resilience among students.

Budgetary limitations also impact the hiring and retention of qualified mental health professionals. Low salaries and high workloads in campus counseling centers make it difficult to attract and retain skilled staff, leading to high turnover rates and staffing shortages. These shortages directly affect students, as wait times for appointments grow longer and the availability of specialized care diminishes. For example, students seeking treatment for trauma or eating disorders may find that their campus lacks the necessary expertise, forcing them to seek care off-campus at higher costs and with logistical challenges.

Despite these challenges, some institutions have made strides in addressing the mental health crisis through innovative programs. Peer support networks, where trained student mentors provide emotional support to their peers, have gained traction as cost-effective tools to reduce stigma and increase access to care. Mental health awareness campaigns, often led by student organizations or counseling centers, aim to normalize conversations about mental health and encourage help-seeking behavior. Partnerships with telehealth providers have also emerged as a promising strategy, particularly in the wake of the COVID-19 pandemic, allowing institutions to extend their reach and provide more flexible care options.

However, these initiatives, while valuable, often fall short of addressing systemic gaps in care. Peer support programs, for example, may not have the training or resources to handle severe or complex mental health issues. Telehealth services, though effective for many, require robust technological infrastructure and may not be accessible to students without reliable internet or private spaces. These limitations highlight the need for more comprehensive and sustainable solutions that go beyond short-term fixes and address the root causes of the mental health crisis.

To create lasting change, colleges must prioritize mental health funding as a central component of their institutional budgets, rather than treating it as a secondary concern. This shift requires a cultural and administrative commitment to integrating mental health into the broader framework of student success, recognizing that well-being is essential to academic and personal achievement.

Links Between Academic Pressures, Debt, and Student Well-Being

The mental health crisis on college campuses cannot be fully understood without examining the interconnected effects of academic pressures and financial stress. These two factors are among the most significant contributors to chronic stress, anxiety, and depression among students, creating a cycle of distress that undermines both mental health and academic performance.

The Impact of Academic Pressures

The academic demands of higher education foster a competitive environment that places immense pressure on students to excel. Rigorous coursework, high-stakes exams, and the expectation to maintain strong grades can create a relentless drive for perfectionism, leaving students with little room for failure or self-compassion. According to the Healthy Minds Network, over 60% of college students report feeling overwhelming anxiety about their academic performance, with many identifying fear of failure as a primary source of stress (Eisenberg et al., 2019).

External pressures from parents, peers, and future employers further exacerbate these challenges. Parents may emphasize the importance of academic success as a gateway to career opportunities, while social comparisons with peers can intensify feelings of inadequacy or imposter syndrome. The job market adds another layer of stress, as students feel compelled to build impressive resumes through internships, leadership roles, and extracurricular activities, often at the expense of their mental health.

The result is a cycle of chronic stress that takes a significant toll on students' well-being. Persistent stress can impair cognitive functioning, making it difficult for students to concentrate, retain information, or perform well academically. Sleep disruptions, a common consequence of academic stress, further exacerbate these challenges, as inadequate rest negatively impacts both physical and mental health. Over time, this cycle can lead to burnout, a state of emotional, physical, and mental exhaustion that leaves students feeling disconnected from their academic and personal goals.

For students who struggle academically, the psychological consequences can be profound. Feelings of shame, inadequacy, and self-doubt may erode their confidence and motivation, creating a downward spiral that affects every aspect of their lives. These struggles often go unnoticed or unaddressed, as students may hesitate to seek help due to stigma or a fear of being perceived as weak.

Addressing the Interconnected Challenges

To address the mental health challenges stemming from academic pressures and financial stress, institutions must adopt a holistic approach that considers the root causes of these issues. This includes promoting a culture of balance and well-being, expanding access to mental health resources, and creating systems that reduce unnecessary stressors while supporting student resilience. By tackling the systemic and cultural factors that contribute to the crisis, colleges can better support their students' academic and emotional success.

Financial Stress and Student Debt

Financial stress is one of the most significant contributors to the mental health crisis among college students, driven by the escalating costs of higher education and the widespread reliance on student loans. The rising expenses associated with tuition, housing, textbooks, and other living costs have left many students burdened with substantial debt. According to the Institute for College Access and Success (TICAS), the average student loan debt for graduates in 2021 was $28,950, with many students borrowing additional funds to cover basic living expenses (TICAS, 2021). This financial burden disproportionately affects low-income and first-generation students, who often lack family resources or safety nets to mitigate the impact of these costs.

The Psychological Toll of Debt

The mental health consequences of student debt are well-documented, with numerous studies highlighting its link to anxiety, depression, and other psychological challenges. Walsemann et al. (2015) found that individuals with high levels of student debt are significantly more likely to experience chronic stress and even suicidal ideation. This relationship underscores the dual pressures of managing current financial obligations and anticipating long-term repayment challenges, which can feel overwhelming for many students.

The psychological toll of debt is not limited to low-income students. Even those from middle-income families report heightened stress as they navigate the complexities of borrowing, budgeting, and planning for the future. The book *The Debt Trap* by Josh Mitchell provides a detailed examination of how student loans have become a pervasive source of financial insecurity, describing the systemic factors that have led to the current crisis. Mitchell emphasizes that the psychological strain of debt is compounded by a lack of transparency in loan terms, insufficient financial education, and the aggressive marketing of loans to vulnerable students, all of which contribute to a sense of entrapment and despair (Mitchell, 2021).

The Impact of Part-Time Work

Many students attempt to alleviate financial stress by working part-time jobs, but this strategy often introduces additional challenges. While employment can provide much-needed income, it also requires significant time and energy, which can detract from academic and personal pursuits. Research shows that students who work more than 20 hours per week are at higher risk of burnout, academic underperformance, and physical health issues (Perna, 2018). For students already grappling with financial insecurity, the demands of balancing work and school can exacerbate feelings of exhaustion and helplessness.

Long-Term Implications

The long-term implications of student debt extend far beyond graduation. Graduates burdened by loans often delay major life milestones, such as purchasing a home, starting a family, or pursuing advanced degrees, due to the financial strain of repayment. These delays can contribute to a sense of stagnation and dissatisfaction, further eroding mental well-being. Mitchell (2021) argues that this cycle of debt and delayed economic participation not only impacts individuals but also has broader societal consequences, as it reduces consumer spending, homeownership rates, and overall economic mobility.

The compounding nature of financial stress, academic demands, and the pressures of part-time work highlights the urgent need for systemic reforms. Institutions must prioritize financial literacy programs, expand access to need-based aid, and advocate for policy changes that reduce the burden of student debt. Without these interventions, the mental health crisis on college campuses will continue to deepen, leaving students to navigate an increasingly precarious financial and emotional landscape.

The Role of Institutional Support

Addressing the intertwined challenges of academic pressures, financial stress, and mental health requires a comprehensive and multifaceted approach. Colleges and universities have a critical responsibility to create environments that not only foster academic excellence but also prioritize the well-being of their students. Institutional support plays a key role in mitigating stressors, reducing stigma, and ensuring that all students have access to the resources and policies necessary to thrive both academically and personally.

Policy Innovations to Alleviate Stressors

Institutions can implement policies that directly address the sources of student stress. Flexible academic policies, such as extended deadlines, pass/fail grading options, and accommodations for students

116

experiencing mental health challenges, can alleviate the pressure to perform under rigid conditions. These policies recognize that students' well-being is integral to their academic success and provide a safety net for those navigating difficult circumstances.

Financial aid policies also play a crucial role in reducing stress. Expanding access to need-based scholarships and emergency grants can provide immediate relief for students facing unexpected expenses, such as medical bills or housing insecurity. Emergency aid programs, which offer quick, small-scale financial assistance, have proven effective in preventing students from dropping out due to short-term financial crises (Goldrick-Rab et al., 2020). Additionally, increasing the availability of on-campus employment opportunities allows students to earn money in ways that are compatible with their academic schedules, reducing the need to take on exhausting off-campus jobs.

Loan forgiveness or income-based repayment programs, when implemented at the institutional level, can also have a profound impact. While these solutions often require collaboration with state and federal policymakers, colleges can advocate for reforms that alleviate the long-term financial burdens of student debt, thereby addressing one of the root causes of chronic financial stress.

Expanding Access to Mental Health Resources

Robust mental health resources are essential to creating a supportive campus environment. Institutions should prioritize expanding counseling services to meet growing demand, ensuring that students have timely access to professional help. This includes hiring more counselors, diversifying staff to reflect the cultural and linguistic needs of the student body, and offering specialized care for conditions such as trauma, eating disorders, and substance abuse.

Telehealth services have emerged as a valuable tool for increasing access to care, particularly for students who may face barriers such as transportation or scheduling conflicts. By partnering with telehealth providers, institutions can offer flexible and confidential support options, enabling students to seek help in ways that fit their unique circumstances. Peer counseling programs also complement professional services by providing students with relatable, accessible support networks.

Reducing Stigma and Fostering a Compassionate Culture

Addressing the mental health crisis on campuses requires a cultural shift toward compassion and understanding. Institutions must lead efforts to destigmatize mental health issues by promoting awareness campaigns, integrating mental health education into orientation programs, and training faculty and staff to recognize signs of distress. Peer-led initiatives, such as student mental health advocacy groups, can play a significant role in normalizing conversations about mental health and encouraging help-seeking behavior.

Faculty and staff training is particularly critical. Professors and academic advisors often serve as the first point of contact for students in distress, and equipping them with the skills to provide support—or direct students to appropriate resources—can make a significant difference. Institutions should offer workshops that educate faculty on mental health issues, fostering an environment where students feel comfortable discussing their challenges.

Tackling Systemic Causes of Stress

Beyond individual interventions, institutions must address the systemic factors contributing to student distress. Academic workloads should be evaluated to ensure they are challenging without being overwhelming. Policies that promote work-life balance, such as designated "mental health days" or reduced class loads during particularly demanding periods, can help students recharge and maintain their well-being.

In addition, institutions can reframe the culture of achievement that often fuels perfectionism and burnout. By emphasizing personal growth, learning for its own sake, and the value of diverse paths to success, colleges can reduce the pressure students feel to conform to narrow definitions of achievement. Career services can also play a role by helping students navigate post-graduation plans in ways that align with their values and long-term goals, reducing the anxiety associated with uncertain futures.

The Long-Term Impact of Institutional Support

The mental health crisis on college campuses is a complex issue that demands immediate and sustained action. By investing in mental health resources, implementing policies that prioritize well-being, and addressing systemic causes of stress, institutions can create healthier, more inclusive learning environments. These changes not only improve individual outcomes—such as academic success, retention, and graduation rates—but also contribute to the overall resilience of the campus community.

Moreover, institutions that prioritize mental health send a powerful message about the importance of compassion and understanding in education. As students graduate and enter the workforce, the skills and habits they develop in these supportive environments—such as seeking help, practicing self-care, and fostering healthy relationships— will serve them throughout their lives. By tackling the root causes of distress and fostering a culture of well-being, colleges and universities can empower future generations to thrive both personally and professionally.

Chapter 13

Reimagining Colleges and Universities

As higher education faces mounting challenges, including economic pressures, shifts in workforce demands, and growing skepticism about its value, there is an urgent need to rethink how colleges and universities function. This chapter explores strategies for reshaping these institutions to better align with societal and market needs, focusing on universities, colleges, and the future of community colleges.

Universities

Universities have traditionally been the epicenters of intellectual exploration and innovation, driving advancements in science, technology, culture, and society. They are where groundbreaking ideas are developed and where the future workforce is educated. However, the rapidly changing landscape of global economies, societal challenges, and workforce demands necessitates a recalibration of university priorities. As the world grapples with issues such as climate change, technological disruption, and widening inequality, universities must evolve to remain relevant and impactful. This evolution involves reorienting research priorities to address pressing societal needs, tackling the oversupply of PhD graduates, and fostering robust partnerships with industry to bridge the gap between academia and practical innovation.

Shifting the Focus of Research to Address Societal Needs

Universities are uniquely positioned to address global challenges through research, yet much of the academic output remains disconnected from real-world applications. Critics argue that the emphasis on theoretical work, often driven by the pressure to publish in prestigious journals, limits the practical utility of university research. While basic research is essential for long-term innovation, there is a growing need for applied research that directly addresses societal challenges such as climate change, public health, urbanization, and food security.

Redirecting research priorities requires a cultural and structural shift within universities. Funding agencies and university leadership can play a pivotal role by incentivizing interdisciplinary research centers that focus on solving specific societal problems. For instance, universities could establish dedicated institutes for renewable energy, artificial intelligence ethics, or pandemic preparedness, aligning their intellectual resources with public needs. Collaborative funding models, where private and public sectors pool resources to support targeted research, can further enhance the societal impact of academic work (Geiger, 2017).

Moreover, universities can integrate community engagement into their research agenda. By partnering with local governments, non-profits, and grassroots organizations, universities can ensure their research has a tangible impact on the communities they serve. These partnerships can also enrich the academic experience for students, exposing them to the complexities of real-world problem-solving.

Addressing the Oversupply of PhD Graduates

One of the most significant challenges facing universities today is the oversupply of PhD graduates relative to the demand for academic positions. While the pursuit of a PhD is often framed as a pathway to intellectual and professional advancement, the reality is that the academic job market is saturated. In the United States, only about 25% of PhD graduates secure tenure-track positions within three years of earning their degree (National Science Foundation, 2021). Many graduates end up in precarious adjunct roles, which offer low pay, minimal job security, and limited opportunities for career growth.

To address this issue, universities must reassess the scale and structure of their doctoral programs. Admissions to PhD programs should be aligned with labor market demands, ensuring that the number of graduates reflects the availability of academic and industry positions. At the same time, PhD curricula should be reimagined to include skills that are applicable beyond academia, such as project management, leadership, data analysis, and communication.

Professional doctorates, such as those in education (EdD) or engineering (DEng), offer an alternative to traditional PhD programs by focusing on practical applications rather than theoretical research. Expanding these types of programs can help align doctoral education with workforce needs while providing students with diverse career pathways (Cassuto, 2021).

Universities can also collaborate with industry partners to create career development programs for PhD students. These programs could include internships, industry-sponsored research projects, and mentorship opportunities, preparing graduates to transition into roles outside academia. By broadening the scope of doctoral education, universities can ensure that their graduates are equipped to contribute meaningfully to society, regardless of their career trajectory.

Fostering Partnerships Between Academia and Industry for Practical Innovation

The disconnect between academia and industry has long been a barrier to the practical application of university research. Universities often focus on theoretical innovation, while industries prioritize immediate problem-solving and product development. Bridging this gap requires closer collaboration between academic institutions and private sector entities, enabling both to benefit from each other's strengths.

One approach is the establishment of innovation hubs or research parks that bring together faculty, students, and industry professionals to collaborate on projects. These hubs can serve as incubators for new technologies and business ideas, accelerating the commercialization of academic research. For example, Stanford University's close ties with Silicon Valley have fostered countless successful startups and innovations, demonstrating the potential of academia-industry collaboration (Etzkowitz, 2008).

Technology transfer offices (TTOs) within universities can also play a crucial role in facilitating partnerships. These offices help researchers navigate the complexities of intellectual property, patents, and licensing, ensuring that their innovations reach the market. Strengthening TTOs and providing them with adequate resources can enhance the impact of university research on the economy and society.

Another avenue for collaboration is through curriculum development. Universities can work with industry partners to design programs that align with workforce needs, ensuring that graduates possess the skills required in high-demand fields. Cooperative education programs, where students alternate between academic study and paid work placements, provide valuable experiential learning opportunities while building strong ties between universities and employers.

Universities stand at a crossroads, facing the dual challenge of preserving their traditional role as centers of intellectual inquiry while adapting to meet the evolving needs of society and the economy. By reorienting research to address pressing societal challenges, restructuring PhD programs to align with labor market realities, and fostering dynamic partnerships with industry, universities can ensure their continued relevance and impact. These changes will not only enhance the value of higher education but also position universities as critical drivers of innovation and societal progress in the 21st century.

Reorienting Research to Address Societal Needs

Academic research is one of the defining features of universities, fueling innovation, informing policy, and advancing societal progress. However, the current research landscape often prioritizes theoretical explorations or niche studies, driven by a publish-or-perish culture that values academic prestige over practical outcomes. While theoretical research plays an essential role in long-term innovation, the growing complexity of global challenges—such as climate change, public health crises, and economic inequality—demands a more focused effort to produce actionable solutions. Critics argue that universities must redirect their research efforts toward addressing these urgent societal needs.

Prioritizing Real-World Challenges

Universities can play a critical role in addressing global and local challenges by aligning their research priorities with societal needs. For instance, climate change mitigation requires research into renewable energy technologies, carbon capture systems, and sustainable urban planning. Public health crises such as the COVID-19 pandemic highlight the need for interdisciplinary research in virology, epidemiology, and healthcare delivery systems. Economic inequality, another pressing issue, can benefit from studies in education access, workforce development, and social policy reform.

Granting agencies such as the National Science Foundation (NSF) and the National Institutes of Health (NIH) can incentivize this shift by prioritizing funding for interdisciplinary projects that address real-world problems. For example, the NSF's "Growing Convergence Research" initiative specifically supports collaborative efforts to tackle complex societal challenges, such as water scarcity or cybersecurity (Geiger, 2017). Similarly, the NIH's focus on translational research bridges the gap between laboratory discoveries and practical applications in healthcare, ensuring that scientific advancements benefit communities in tangible ways.

Universities themselves can reinforce this focus by establishing specialized research centers dedicated to societal challenges. Centers for sustainability, renewable energy, mental health, or urban resilience can concentrate resources and expertise on critical issues, fostering innovation while addressing community needs. For instance, Stanford University's Precourt Institute for Energy is a leading example of how academic institutions can drive advancements in renewable energy through targeted research.

Restructuring the Peer-Review and Publication Process

The peer-review and publication process, a cornerstone of academic research, currently emphasizes theoretical novelty and publication quantity over practical impact. This system can discourage researchers from pursuing applied projects, as journals with higher prestige often prioritize theoretical contributions. To realign research incentives, universities and journals must adopt new metrics that value societal impact.

Universities could establish internal evaluation criteria that assess the real-world benefits of research projects. For example, faculty performance reviews could consider metrics such as community engagement, policy influence, or industry partnerships alongside traditional measures like publication count and citation impact. These changes would encourage researchers to prioritize work that addresses societal needs without compromising academic rigor.

Similarly, academic journals could introduce special sections or dedicated issues for research with practical applications. By providing platforms for applied research, journals can validate the importance of this work and ensure it reaches a broader audience, including policymakers, industry leaders, and non-academic stakeholders.

Encouraging Interdisciplinary Collaboration

Addressing complex societal challenges requires a collaborative, interdisciplinary approach. Many pressing issues, such as climate change or public health, lie at the intersection of multiple disciplines.

Universities can foster interdisciplinary collaboration by breaking down departmental silos and creating opportunities for cross-disciplinary research teams. Joint appointments for faculty, interdisciplinary graduate programs, and shared research facilities can encourage collaboration and innovation.

Programs such as the University of Oxford's Environmental Change Institute exemplify how interdisciplinary research can drive meaningful change. By bringing together experts from environmental science, economics, public policy, and social sciences, the institute develops comprehensive solutions to sustainability challenges. Similar models can be adopted by universities worldwide to maximize the impact of their research.

Engaging Communities and Stakeholders

For research to have a tangible societal impact, universities must engage with the communities and stakeholders who will benefit from their findings. Community-based participatory research (CBPR) is a valuable model that involves stakeholders in the research process, ensuring that projects address real-world needs and incorporate local knowledge. For example, universities partnering with local governments on urban development projects can create data-driven policies that improve infrastructure, reduce inequality, and enhance quality of life.

Stakeholder engagement also extends to industry collaborations. Universities can work with private sector partners to identify research priorities, develop innovative solutions, and accelerate the translation of discoveries into products or services. Such partnerships not only amplify the impact of academic research but also provide opportunities for funding, internships, and technology transfer.

Reorienting research to address societal needs is essential for universities to remain relevant and impactful in an increasingly complex world. By prioritizing real-world challenges, restructuring the peer-review process, fostering interdisciplinary collaboration, and engaging with communities and stakeholders, universities can ensure that their research contributes to solving pressing global issues. These changes require a cultural and structural shift within academia, but the potential benefits—for society, industry, and the academic community—are immense. Through these efforts, universities can reaffirm their role as engines of progress and innovation, bridging the gap between knowledge creation and societal transformation.

Limiting the Production of PhD Graduates to Match Job Market Demands

The academic job market has failed to keep pace with the exponential growth in the number of PhD graduates, leading to an oversaturated market where supply far exceeds demand. This imbalance has resulted in a surplus of highly educated individuals vying for a shrinking pool of tenure-track positions. In 2019, fewer than 25% of PhD graduates in the United States secured tenure-track roles within three years of earning their degree, leaving many in precarious adjunct roles with low pay, limited job security, and minimal benefits (National Science Foundation, 2021). Others leave academia entirely, often finding themselves overqualified for non-academic roles or struggling to adapt their skills to industry demands.

Aligning PhD Admissions with Job Market Realities

To address this imbalance, universities must align PhD admissions with job market realities. Graduate programs often admit far more students than the academic job market can absorb, driven in part by institutional incentives to attract research funding and enhance prestige. Universities should adopt more strategic admissions practices, taking into account labor market trends, industry needs, and the availability of academic positions. This approach would help ensure that the number of PhD graduates is commensurate with demand, reducing underemployment and the devaluation of advanced degrees.

Additionally, institutions should encourage transparency about career prospects for prospective and current PhD students. Programs could provide data on job placement rates, median time to degree completion, and career outcomes for alumni. This information would enable students to make more informed decisions about pursuing a doctorate and help set realistic expectations for their post-graduation prospects.

Restructuring Doctoral Programs for Versatility

Traditional PhD programs often emphasize academic research and teaching, leaving graduates underprepared for roles outside academia. To enhance the versatility of doctoral education, universities should integrate professional development opportunities and skills training into their curricula. Courses in project management, data analysis, entrepreneurship, and science communication can equip students with competencies that are highly valued in industry and government sectors.

Professional doctorates, such as those in education (EdD), engineering (DEng), and public health (DrPH), offer an alternative to traditional PhD programs. These degrees focus on the application of knowledge to real-world problems, making graduates more competitive in non-academic job markets (Cassuto, 2021). Expanding professional doctoral programs and promoting them as viable alternatives can help align graduate education with workforce needs.

Collaborative Strategies for Graduate Education Reform

Universities should collaborate with policymakers, funding agencies, and industry leaders to develop comprehensive strategies for reforming graduate education. Regional or national frameworks could help coordinate efforts to balance the production of PhD graduates with societal and economic needs. For example, funding agencies could incentivize programs that incorporate industry partnerships or prioritize fields with high labor market demand, such as healthcare, technology, and renewable energy.

Universities could also establish career development offices dedicated to graduate students, providing resources for job placement, networking, and skills training. Partnerships with industry and government organizations can create internship opportunities, mentorship programs, and applied research projects, helping students gain valuable experience and expand their career options.

Encouraging Partnerships Between Academia and Industry for Practical Innovation

Universities have long been engines of innovation, generating knowledge that drives scientific and technological progress. However, the disconnect between academic research and industry applications often hinders the practical impact of their work. Strengthening partnerships between academia and industry is essential to accelerate the translation of research into real-world solutions, fostering economic growth and addressing societal challenges.

Establishing Innovation Hubs and Research Collaborations

Innovation hubs are one of the most effective ways to facilitate collaboration between academia and industry. These centers bring together faculty, students, and industry professionals to work on joint projects that address specific challenges. By pooling resources and expertise, innovation hubs can accelerate the development of new technologies, products, and processes. For example, MIT's Innovation Initiative has successfully created partnerships with companies in fields such as artificial intelligence, clean energy, and biotechnology, driving both academic advancement and commercial success.

Research collaborations can also take the form of joint funding initiatives, where universities and industry partners co-invest in projects with shared goals. Such collaborations ensure that research aligns with market needs while leveraging the unique strengths of both academia and industry.

The Role of Technology Transfer Offices

Technology transfer offices (TTOs) play a critical role in bridging the gap between academic research and industry applications. These offices assist researchers in navigating intellectual property issues, securing patents, and licensing technologies to companies. By providing support for commercialization, TTOs help ensure that academic discoveries reach the marketplace, where they can benefit society.

For example, Stanford University's Office of Technology Licensing has facilitated the commercialization of numerous groundbreaking innovations, including the Google search algorithm and DNA sequencing technologies. Strengthening TTOs and providing them with adequate resources can enhance the societal and economic impact of university research (Etzkowitz, 2008).

Enhancing Student Employability Through Industry Partnerships

Internships, cooperative education programs, and industry-sponsored research projects are valuable tools for integrating students into the private sector. These initiatives provide students with hands-on experience, enabling them to apply their academic knowledge to practical problems. For example, cooperative education programs allow students to alternate between academic study and full-time employment, giving them a deeper understanding of industry needs while earning a salary.

Such partnerships also benefit industry, which gains access to a pipeline of talented, well-trained individuals who are familiar with their operations. For students, these experiences improve employability, expand professional networks, and often lead to job offers after graduation. Universities can formalize these collaborations through agreements with industry partners, ensuring a steady flow of opportunities for their students.

Reforming PhD programs to align with job market demands and strengthening academia-industry partnerships are critical steps in reimagining the role of universities. By limiting the production of PhD graduates to match labor market realities and equipping them with versatile skills, universities can ensure that doctoral education remains a valuable and sustainable endeavor. At the same time, fostering closer ties with industry through innovation hubs, technology transfer offices, and experiential learning opportunities will enhance the practical impact of academic research. These reforms will not only benefit universities and their graduates but also contribute to economic growth and societal progress.

Colleges are Central to Opportunity and Adaptation

Colleges, particularly those offering associate and bachelor's degrees, play a vital role in the U.S. higher education system, serving as accessible gateways to economic opportunity and social mobility. These institutions cater to diverse student populations, including working adults, first-generation students, and underserved communities, making them integral to addressing workforce needs and regional economic development. However, as economic realities, workforce demands, and student demographics shift, colleges must adapt by expanding workforce-aligned programs, improving transfer pathways, and supporting student success through innovative reforms and partnerships.

Despite their essential contributions, colleges—especially community colleges—face significant resistance from doctoral-degree-granting universities, which often marginalize and undermine efforts by these institutions to offer bachelor's degrees. This tension highlights broader structural challenges within the higher education system and the need to address systemic inequities that limit the full potential of colleges to serve their communities.

Expanding Bachelor's Degrees in Industry-Aligned Fields

In response to the growing demand for advanced skills in the labor market, many community colleges have begun offering bachelor's degrees in applied and technical fields. These programs are specifically designed to meet regional workforce needs, focusing on areas like healthcare, information technology, education, and advanced manufacturing. Unlike traditional four-year university programs, these bachelor's degrees emphasize hands-on training and direct career pathways, providing students with affordable and accessible opportunities to achieve upward mobility.

For example, institutions like Miami Dade College and the College of Southern Nevada have successfully implemented bachelor's programs tailored to meet local economic demands, addressing critical labor shortages in industries such as nursing, cybersecurity, and business management. These programs are particularly valuable for nontraditional students who may not have the financial means or flexibility to attend a four-year university.

However, many doctoral-degree-granting universities actively resist these efforts, citing concerns about mission creep and competition for students. Critics argue that this resistance is often motivated by a desire to maintain institutional prestige and monopolize bachelor's degree offerings. By lobbying policymakers and accrediting agencies, universities have attempted to limit the ability of community colleges to offer bachelor's degrees, often delaying program approvals or imposing additional regulatory hurdles.

The Politics of Marginalization

The opposition from universities has created significant barriers for colleges seeking to expand their bachelor's degree offerings. Doctoral institutions often argue that allowing community colleges to offer bachelor's degrees dilutes the perceived quality of higher education and encroaches on their traditional domain. These arguments, however, ignore the practical realities of student needs and regional workforce demands.

Research shows that community college bachelor's programs are not only effective in preparing students for high-demand jobs but also serve populations that are less likely to attend traditional universities, such as working adults and low-income students (Miller & Erwin, 2020). The resistance from universities has led to an uneven playing field, where community colleges must navigate a patchwork of state policies and opposition from entrenched interests to justify their programs.

For instance, in California, efforts by community colleges to expand bachelor's degree programs have faced significant pushback from the state's university systems, delaying approvals and restricting the scope of potential programs. Similarly, in other states, doctoral universities have used their influence to lobby against legislation that would enable community colleges to meet growing workforce demands through bachelor's degrees.

The Case for Equity and Collaboration

The tension between colleges and universities reflects broader inequities in the higher education system, where institutional prestige often takes precedence over accessibility and workforce alignment. To address these challenges, policymakers must create equitable frameworks that empower colleges to fulfill their missions without unnecessary interference.

Expanding community college bachelor's programs offers a pragmatic solution to addressing workforce gaps and increasing educational attainment, particularly in underserved regions. Collaborative models, where universities and colleges partner to offer joint programs or share resources, can help bridge the divide while ensuring that students have access to a range of affordable, high-quality options.

Supporting Student Success Through Systemic Change

As colleges expand their offerings and navigate systemic resistance, they must also prioritize comprehensive support systems to ensure student success. Many students face barriers such as financial insecurity, academic underpreparedness, and family responsibilities, which can impede their ability to complete their degrees. Addressing these challenges requires a multifaceted approach:

1. Workforce-Aligned Programs: Expanding applied bachelor's degrees in high-demand fields ensures that students gain the skills and credentials needed to succeed in today's economy.

2. Transfer Pathways: Streamlined articulation agreements with universities can help students transition seamlessly from associate to bachelor's programs, minimizing credit loss and time to degree completion.

3. Holistic Support Services: Colleges must invest in financial aid, mental health counseling, childcare, and career services to address the diverse needs of their student populations.

4. Advocacy for Policy Reform: Colleges must work with policymakers to challenge systemic inequities and advocate for the expansion of bachelor's degree programs as a critical tool for workforce development and social mobility.

Colleges are uniquely positioned to address the evolving needs of students and the workforce, but systemic barriers and institutional politics often hinder their ability to innovate and expand. By prioritizing workforce alignment, improving student support systems, and challenging the resistance from doctoral-degree-granting universities, colleges can continue to serve as engines of economic opportunity and social equity. Empowering colleges to offer bachelor's degrees in applied fields is not just a matter of meeting labor market demands; it is an essential step toward creating a more inclusive and effective higher education system.

Streamlining Workforce-Focused Programs to Align with Market Needs

The modern economy requires a workforce equipped with specialized skills, yet many college programs fail to adequately prepare graduates for high-demand fields. Healthcare, information technology, renewable energy, and advanced manufacturing are examples of sectors experiencing rapid growth, yet many colleges continue to offer outdated or mismatched programs that do not align with these industries.

To address this gap, colleges should regularly conduct labor market analyses to identify regional and national employment trends. These analyses can inform the development of new programs and the revision of existing curricula to ensure alignment with employer needs. For instance, colleges in areas with a growing demand for clean energy technicians could introduce or expand programs in solar panel installation, wind turbine maintenance, and energy auditing.

Collaborations with local employers and industry groups are vital to this process. Establishing advisory boards comprising industry leaders can help colleges design relevant curricula and identify key skills that graduates need to succeed in the workforce. Internships, apprenticeships, and cooperative education programs provide students with hands-on experience while fostering strong connections between colleges and employers. These partnerships not only enhance students' employability but also create pipelines for graduates to transition seamlessly into full-time positions.

Moreover, colleges should prioritize stackable credentials—programs that allow students to earn certifications or associate degrees that can later be applied toward higher degrees. This approach provides flexibility for working adults and nontraditional students, enabling them to build their qualifications incrementally while remaining competitive in the job market.

Phasing Out Low-Value Certificates and Improving Transfer Pathways

One of the most significant inefficiencies in higher education is the prevalence of low-value certificates—short-term programs that fail to lead to meaningful employment or wage increases. These programs represent a poor return on investment for both students and institutions, often leaving graduates with credentials that hold little to no value in the job market. This not only wastes student time and financial resources but also diverts institutional efforts away from initiatives that could have a greater impact on student outcomes and economic mobility.

The Problem with Low-Value Certificates

Community colleges are often quick to introduce certifications across a wide range of fields, frequently without adequately evaluating their relevance to labor market demands. The ease with which new certifications are added is not matched by an equally rigorous process for eliminating underperforming programs. As a result, many colleges continue to offer certifications with little or no value, leading students to earn credentials that do not translate into meaningful employment opportunities or wage increases.

This proliferation of low-value certificates can be attributed to several factors. First, adding new programs allows colleges to appeal to a broader range of potential students and demonstrate responsiveness to perceived workforce needs. However, without proper data analysis and stakeholder input, these programs often fail to align with actual job market demands. Second, once programs are established, institutional inertia and political pressures from faculty, local stakeholders, or advisory boards can make it difficult to terminate them, even when they consistently fail to produce positive outcomes for students.

For students, the consequences of earning low-value certificates can be profound. Many graduate with the expectation that their credential will lead to better job prospects or higher wages, only to find that employers do not value the certification or that the skills acquired are insufficient for employment in their desired field. This mismatch can lead to frustration, wasted financial resources, and even disillusionment with higher education.

The Need for Data-Driven Program Assessment

To address this issue, colleges must adopt a data-driven approach to identifying and phasing out low-value certificates. By leveraging metrics such as graduate employment rates, median wages, job satisfaction, and alignment with regional labor market needs, institutions can assess the effectiveness of their programs. Programs that consistently fail to produce positive outcomes should be restructured or eliminated to free up resources for more impactful initiatives.

The use of outcome data can also help colleges avoid introducing unnecessary programs in the first place. Collaborating with local employers, industry groups, and workforce development agencies can provide valuable insights into the skills and credentials that are most in demand. Establishing a regular review process for all certificate programs ensures that offerings remain relevant and aligned with evolving labor market trends.

Improving Transfer Pathways

In addition to addressing low-value certificates, improving transfer pathways between community colleges and four-year institutions is critical to maximizing the value of higher education. Many community college students intend to pursue a bachelor's degree but face significant challenges transferring their credits to four-year institutions. These barriers often result in lost credits, extended time to degree completion, increased costs, and higher dropout rates.

Research shows that fewer than 15% of community college students who start with the intention of earning a bachelor's degree succeed in doing so within six years, largely due to credit transfer issues (Jenkins

& Fink, 2016). The current patchwork of articulation agreements, transfer policies, and inconsistent credit evaluations creates a labyrinthine process for students, leaving them to navigate unclear and often incompatible academic pathways. This inefficiency undermines the purpose of community colleges as a cost-effective starting point for higher education.

The Case for Fundamental Structural Reform

While solutions like streamlined articulation agreements, dual-admission programs, and shared advising systems provide temporary relief, they fail to address the root cause of transfer inefficiencies: the separation of community colleges and four-year universities. The only way to truly resolve these challenges is through a structural overhaul of the higher education system.

One approach is to eliminate community colleges as standalone two-year institutions and integrate them into university systems. Under this model, community colleges would function as lower-division campuses of a larger university system, ensuring seamless transitions between associate and bachelor's degree programs. This integration would eliminate credit loss entirely, as students would remain within the same institution throughout their academic journey. Faculty alignment, unified curriculum standards, and centralized advising systems would further enhance the student experience, making it easier to progress from one stage to the next without bureaucratic obstacles.

Alternatively, community colleges could evolve into standalone bachelor's degree-granting institutions, similar to models already implemented in states like Florida and Washington. By expanding their capacity to offer four-year degrees, community colleges would eliminate the need for students to transfer altogether. These bachelor's programs would focus on applied and workforce-aligned fields, providing students with affordable, accessible pathways to high-demand careers.

Benefits of Integration or Transformation

The benefits of integrating community colleges into university systems or transitioning them to bachelor's degree-granting institutions are manifold:

1. **Elimination of Credit Loss**: Students would no longer face the frustration of discovering that their hard-earned credits do not transfer to their desired program. Unified systems ensure that every course counts toward degree completion.

2. **Reduced Time and Cost**: Without the delays caused by transfer barriers, students could complete their degrees more efficiently, reducing tuition expenses and the opportunity costs associated with extended enrollment.

3. **Enhanced Academic and Career Support**: Integrated systems provide access to a broader range of resources, such as university-level libraries, career services, and research opportunities, improving both academic outcomes and career readiness.

4. **Increased Equity and Access**: By eliminating the transfer barrier, these reforms would particularly benefit first-generation, low-income, and nontraditional students, who are disproportionately affected by the inefficiencies of the current system.

5. **Workforce Alignment**: Standalone bachelor's degree-granting community colleges could tailor their programs to regional economic needs, directly addressing labor shortages in fields such as healthcare, technology, and education.

Dual-Admission Programs as a Transitional Solution

While structural reforms may take time to implement, dual-admission programs can serve as an interim strategy to improve transfer pathways. Under these programs, students are simultaneously enrolled at a community college and a partnering four-year institution, granting them access to advising, resources, and guarantees of credit transfer from the outset. Programs like California's Transfer Admission Guarantee (TAG) have shown promise in helping students transition smoothly, but they still rely on coordination between separate institutions, leaving room for inconsistencies and inefficiencies.

The Path Forward

Improving transfer pathways is essential to ensuring that higher education fulfills its promise of social mobility and economic opportunity. However, piecemeal reforms are insufficient to address the systemic inefficiencies that undermine student success. Integrating community colleges into university systems or transforming them into standalone bachelor's degree-granting institutions offers a bold and effective solution, eliminating credit loss, reducing costs, and empowering students to achieve their educational and career goals. By embracing these structural changes, policymakers and educators can create a more equitable and efficient higher education system for future generations.

Leveraging Technology to Support Transfers

Investments in technology can further enhance transfer pathways by providing tools to track student progress and facilitate communication between institutions. Digital degree planning platforms can ensure that students understand how their courses will transfer and fit into their desired degree programs. These tools can also help advisors identify potential issues early, allowing students to make informed decisions about their academic paths.

Additionally, statewide transfer databases, such as California's Assist.org or Florida's statewide articulation system, serve as models for simplifying credit transfer and improving transparency. Expanding and refining such systems on a national scale could provide even greater consistency and clarity for students navigating the transfer process.

Addressing the issue of low-value certificates and improving transfer pathways are essential steps in creating a more efficient and equitable higher education system. By phasing out underperforming programs and redirecting resources to workforce-aligned credentials, colleges can ensure that students receive education that translates into meaningful economic mobility. At the same time, investments in streamlined transfer pathways and technological tools can help more students achieve their goals of earning bachelor's degrees. Together, these reforms will enhance the value of higher education, empowering students to succeed in an increasingly complex and competitive job market.

Supporting Student Success Through Holistic Services

To improve retention and graduation rates, colleges must adopt a holistic approach to supporting students. Many students, particularly those from underserved communities, face barriers such as financial insecurity, mental health challenges, and inadequate academic preparation. Addressing these challenges requires comprehensive services that address students' academic, personal, and professional needs.

Financial aid remains a cornerstone of student support, but colleges should expand their offerings to include emergency grants, affordable childcare for student parents, and transportation assistance. Early alert systems that identify at-risk students can connect them with resources before challenges escalate, improving retention rates.

Mental health services are another critical area of investment. The growing mental health crisis on campuses demands that colleges provide accessible counseling and wellness programs. Institutions can also train faculty and staff to recognize signs of distress and direct students to appropriate resources.

Career services play a vital role in bridging the gap between education and employment. Comprehensive career centers that offer resume workshops, mock interviews, and networking events can equip students with the tools they need to succeed in the job market. Partnerships with local businesses can provide internship and job opportunities, ensuring that students graduate with both academic credentials and practical experience.

Colleges are uniquely positioned to prepare students for economic success and personal growth, but they must evolve to meet the demands of a changing world. By streamlining workforce-focused programs, phasing out low-value certificates, improving transfer pathways, and investing in holistic student support, colleges can enhance their relevance and impact. These reforms not only benefit individual students but also strengthen communities and contribute to a more dynamic and equitable economy.

Investing in Holistic Student Support to Increase Retention and Graduation Rates

Student success is a central goal for colleges, but achieving it requires a comprehensive approach that addresses the multifaceted challenges students face. Many students enter college with significant barriers, such as financial insecurity, mental health struggles, and inadequate academic preparation. These obstacles contribute to attrition rates that undermine both student outcomes and institutional effectiveness. To combat this, colleges must invest in holistic support systems that prioritize academic, personal, and professional development. By doing so, they can create an environment where all students have the resources and guidance needed to thrive.

Addressing the Barriers to Student Success

Holistic student support involves recognizing and addressing the diverse factors that influence retention and graduation rates. Financial insecurity remains one of the most significant barriers, as many students struggle to afford tuition, textbooks, and living expenses. Colleges can mitigate this by expanding access to scholarships, grants, and work-study opportunities. Emergency financial aid programs, which provide immediate relief for unexpected expenses, have also proven effective in preventing students from dropping out due to short-term financial crises (Goldrick-Rab et al., 2020).

Mental health challenges are another critical factor affecting retention. The American College Health Association (2021) reports that anxiety, depression, and stress are among the leading reasons students withdraw from college. Investing in accessible mental health counseling, wellness programs, and peer support networks can help students manage these challenges. For example, some colleges have implemented 24/7 telehealth services, allowing students to access mental health support at any time.

Academic preparedness is also a significant concern, particularly for first-generation and nontraditional students. Many struggle with the demands of college-level coursework, which can lead to frustration and disengagement. Academic advising, tutoring, and study skills workshops can provide students with the tools they need to succeed. Additionally, colleges can offer bridge programs or extended orientation sessions to help students transition smoothly into the college environment.

Leveraging Early Alert Systems

Early alert systems are a powerful tool for identifying at-risk students and connecting them with appropriate resources. These systems use data such as attendance records, grades, and participation metrics to flag students who may be struggling. Advisors can then intervene proactively, offering personalized support to address the underlying issues. For example, a student missing multiple classes might be referred to academic counseling or provided with resources to address transportation challenges.

By integrating early alert systems into their student support frameworks, colleges can prevent minor issues from escalating into major barriers. Research shows that early interventions significantly improve retention rates, as they help students feel supported and valued by their institution (Kuh et al., 2011).

Utilizing Technology to Enhance Support

Technology plays a crucial role in modern student support systems, offering scalable and flexible solutions to meet diverse needs. Degree planning software, for instance, allows students to map out their academic pathways, ensuring they take the right courses in the correct sequence to graduate on time. These tools can also highlight prerequisites and potential scheduling conflicts, reducing the risk of delayed graduation.

Online tutoring platforms are another valuable resource, providing students with academic assistance regardless of their location or schedule. These platforms often include features such as real-time chat with tutors, video tutorials, and interactive exercises, making them highly effective for students who may not have access to on-campus resources.

Mobile apps that consolidate support services into a single platform can also enhance accessibility. For example, apps that combine academic advising, financial aid tracking, and mental health resources enable students to access assistance quickly and conveniently. Colleges can further personalize these tools by integrating AI-driven chatbots that provide instant responses to common questions, directing students to the appropriate resources.

The Role of Career Services

Holistic support extends beyond graduation to include career preparation. Career services are essential for helping students transition from college to the workforce, yet they are often underutilized. Colleges should invest in robust career centers that offer resume reviews, mock interviews, job fairs, and networking events. Partnerships with local businesses can create internship opportunities, giving students valuable hands-on experience in their chosen fields.

Moreover, embedding career readiness into the curriculum ensures that all students receive practical training and guidance. For example, requiring students to complete an internship or develop a portfolio as part of their degree program can provide them with a competitive edge in the job market.

Supporting Specific Student Populations

Certain student populations, such as first-generation, low-income, and nontraditional students, face unique challenges that require targeted interventions. First-generation students often lack the familial support and institutional knowledge that can ease the transition to college. Mentorship programs pairing these students with faculty or peers can provide guidance and encouragement.

Nontraditional students, including working adults and parents, may struggle to balance their academic responsibilities with other obligations. Flexible course scheduling, online learning options, and access to childcare can make higher education more accessible for this group. Additionally, creating spaces where these students can connect and share experiences fosters a sense of community and belonging.

Measuring the Impact of Holistic Support

To ensure the effectiveness of their investments, colleges must regularly assess the impact of their support systems. Metrics such as retention rates, graduation rates, and student satisfaction surveys provide valuable insights into what is working and where improvements are needed. Continuous feedback loops, where students can share their experiences and suggestions, are also critical for refining support services.

Investing in holistic student support systems is not only essential for improving retention and graduation rates but also for fostering a more equitable and inclusive higher education system. By addressing financial, academic, and personal barriers, leveraging technology, and tailoring services to meet the needs of diverse student populations, colleges can create an environment where all students have the opportunity to succeed. These efforts benefit not only individual students but also the institutions and communities they serve, ensuring a more resilient and dynamic future for higher education.

The End of Community Colleges

Community colleges have long served as accessible and affordable entry points into higher education, offering students a chance to pursue associate degrees, vocational training, and pathways to four-year institutions. However, as the demands of the workforce evolve and the limitations of the traditional community college model become increasingly apparent, the role of these institutions is being called into question. Low transfer rates, the proliferation of low-value certificates, and systemic inefficiencies have led critics to argue that community colleges, in their current form, have outlived their purpose. To better meet the needs of students and the economy, bold reforms are necessary—whether by integrating community colleges into university systems or transforming them into standalone bachelor's-degree-granting institutions. The time has come to reimagine the community college model to ensure it remains relevant and effective in a rapidly changing world.

Community Colleges Have Outlived Their Purpose

Community colleges were originally established to provide affordable, accessible education to local populations, offering associate degrees, vocational training, and a stepping stone to four-year institutions. However, critics argue that the standalone two-year college model has become outdated in today's rapidly changing educational and economic landscape. While community colleges continue to serve many students, their low transfer rates, limited workforce alignment, and systemic inefficiencies often fail to deliver the social mobility and economic opportunities they promise. Moreover, issues such as chronic underfunding, high student-to-advisor ratios, and the proliferation of low-value certificates have highlighted the need for transformative change in the community college system (Bailey et al., 2015).

The days of standalone community colleges are over. To remain relevant and effective, community colleges must either be integrated into university systems to eliminate credit transfer barriers or transformed into independent bachelor's-degree-granting institutions capable of addressing modern workforce demands. Without such bold reforms, the community college model risks perpetuating inequities and failing to meet the needs of students and the economy.

Migrating Community Colleges into Universities or Elevating Them to Bachelor's-Granting Institutions

The inefficiencies of the traditional community college model have prompted calls for structural reform to align these institutions more closely with the needs of students and employers. Two transformative solutions have emerged: integrating community colleges into existing university systems or transitioning them into standalone bachelor's-degree-granting institutions.

Integration with Universities: A Seamless Pathway

Integrating community colleges into university systems would create a unified framework for higher education, eliminating the transfer barriers that often hinder student progress. In the current system, many community college students who intend to earn a bachelor's degree face significant challenges transferring credits to four-year institutions. These obstacles result in lost time, increased costs, and high dropout rates. Research shows that fewer than 15% of community college students who start with the intention of earning a bachelor's degree succeed in doing so within six years (Jenkins & Fink, 2016).

By integrating community colleges into universities, students would remain within a single institution as they transition from associate to bachelor's programs, ensuring that every credit earned counts toward their degree. This model could also streamline advising, unify faculty and curriculum standards, and provide access to a wider range of resources, such as research facilities, libraries, and career services. Additionally, pooling funding and infrastructure between community colleges and universities would create more efficient systems capable of serving larger and more diverse student populations.

States like California and Texas have experimented with dual-enrollment programs and partnerships between community colleges and universities, but full integration would take these efforts to the next level. A unified system could offer seamless academic and administrative pathways, ensuring that students experience fewer delays and disruptions in their educational journeys.

Transforming Community Colleges into Bachelor's-Granting Institutions

An alternative solution is to transition community colleges into standalone bachelor's-degree-granting institutions. This model, already implemented successfully in states like Florida and Washington, allows community colleges to expand their offerings and provide students with the credentials needed for high-demand careers. By focusing on applied and workforce-aligned fields such as nursing, education, cybersecurity, and advanced manufacturing, these institutions can directly address regional labor shortages while offering affordable, accessible degree options.

Standalone bachelor's programs at community colleges often emphasize practical, hands-on training and partnerships with local employers, ensuring that graduates are job-ready. For example, Miami Dade College and CUNY's bachelor's programs have demonstrated strong outcomes, providing pathways to economic mobility for underserved populations. These institutions have proven that community colleges can effectively meet the demands of the modern workforce while maintaining their commitment to affordability and accessibility.

Transitioning to bachelor's-degree-granting institutions also empowers community colleges to attract and retain students who might otherwise leave for traditional universities. By offering a full range of degree programs, these colleges can serve as comprehensive hubs of education and training, eliminating the need for students to navigate the complexities of transferring to another institution.

The Case for Structural Reform

The traditional community college model, while historically significant, has failed to keep pace with the evolving needs of students and the economy. The separation between community colleges and universities creates systemic inefficiencies that disproportionately affect low-income, first-generation, and nontraditional students. Integrating community colleges into university systems or transitioning them to bachelor's-degree-granting institutions offers a path forward, addressing these challenges while preserving the accessibility and affordability that define community colleges.

These structural reforms would not only eliminate credit transfer barriers but also create more equitable opportunities for students to achieve their educational and career goals. By aligning programs with workforce needs, expanding degree options, and improving resource allocation, reimagined community colleges can become engines of economic mobility and social equity.

A Necessary Evolution

The standalone community college, as it currently exists, is no longer sufficient to meet the demands of today's higher education landscape. Integrating community colleges into universities or transforming them into independent bachelor's-degree-granting institutions is essential to ensuring their relevance and effectiveness. These bold reforms will create a more efficient, equitable, and impactful higher education system, empowering students to succeed in an increasingly complex and competitive world. The time has come to embrace these changes and reimagine community colleges as dynamic institutions capable of driving innovation, workforce development, and social progress.

The transformation of community colleges is not just a necessary evolution—it is an imperative for the future of higher education. The standalone two-year college model, while once revolutionary, has outlived its purpose in addressing the demands of today's workforce and society. By integrating community colleges into university systems or transitioning them into bachelor's-degree-granting institutions, we can eliminate inefficiencies, enhance student outcomes, and create a seamless pathway to success. These bold changes will not only empower students with the skills and credentials they need to thrive but also ensure that higher education fulfills its promise as a catalyst for economic mobility and social equity. The time for incremental reforms has passed; the future of community colleges depends on decisive, transformative action.

Chapter 14

Making Education Affordable Again

E ducation is the cornerstone of opportunity, yet its soaring costs have transformed it into a privilege rather than a right— leaving millions of Americans burdened with debt and dreams deferred. To truly invest in our future, we must reimagine affordability, hold institutions accountable, and ensure that higher education becomes not just accessible, but attainable for all

Proposals for Free or Reduced-Cost Tuition

The escalating cost of higher education in the United States has created an affordability crisis that threatens to undermine the principles of accessibility and inclusivity that higher education should embody. Over the past few decades, tuition fees have risen significantly faster than inflation, leaving many prospective students and families grappling with stark choices: either take on burdensome debt that can take decades to repay or forego higher education entirely. For students from low- and middle-income backgrounds, these financial barriers can perpetuate cycles of inequality, limiting their opportunities for upward mobility and leaving critical workforce gaps in sectors like healthcare, technology, and education. Against this backdrop, free or reduced-cost tuition programs have emerged as a beacon of hope. These programs aim to alleviate financial strain, level the playing field, and equip a diverse range of students with the education needed to thrive in a competitive global economy (Goldrick-Rab, 2016). Free tuition initiatives generally fall into two categories: last-dollar scholarships and first-dollar scholarships, each with distinct advantages and limitations.

Last-Dollar Scholarships

Last-dollar scholarships are structured to bridge the financial gap between a student's existing aid package and the remaining tuition cost. After applying grants, such as Pell Grants, and any other scholarships or financial aid, last-dollar programs step in to cover the balance. This approach allows states to maximize their limited budgets, targeting resources specifically at tuition costs without duplicating other forms of aid. Programs like Tennessee Promise exemplify this model. Tennessee Promise guarantees free community college tuition for high school graduates, making it one of the most prominent examples of a state-driven last-dollar initiative. Since its implementation, Tennessee Promise has significantly increased community college enrollment rates among high school graduates, particularly in rural and underserved communities (Dynarski et al., 2018).

However, last-dollar scholarships are not without criticism. While they eliminate tuition costs, these programs often leave students responsible for other substantial expenses, including textbooks, housing, transportation, and childcare. These costs, sometimes even higher than tuition itself, disproportionately affect low-income students, who may lack the resources to cover these ancillary expenses. Consequently, the financial burden shifts rather than diminishes, creating barriers that still prevent some students from persisting to graduation (Huelsman, 2018).

Moreover, last-dollar programs typically focus on recent high school graduates, excluding many nontraditional students who do not fit the conventional mold of a full-time college attendee. Part-time students, working adults returning to education, and single parents—populations that often represent the most financially vulnerable—are frequently ineligible for these programs. This exclusion undermines the overarching goal of equity and accessibility, as these groups are among those who could benefit the most from reduced tuition costs.

Critics also argue that the design of last-dollar scholarships fails to address systemic challenges within higher education funding. While these programs alleviate some financial pressure, they do not tackle the underlying drivers of rising tuition costs, such as declining state investment in public education, increasing administrative expenses, and the prioritization of amenities over affordability. For these reasons, while last-dollar scholarships are a step in the right direction, they represent a partial solution to the broader affordability crisis.

While last-dollar scholarships demonstrate the potential to expand access to higher education, their limitations highlight the need for more comprehensive approaches that address both direct and indirect costs. By examining the successes and shortcomings of programs like Tennessee Promise, policymakers can refine and expand such initiatives to include nontraditional students, cover ancillary costs, and ensure that financial barriers do not derail students' educational aspirations.

First-Dollar Scholarships

Unlike last-dollar scholarships, first-dollar programs prioritize funding tuition costs upfront, enabling students to use other financial aid for living expenses and reducing overall financial stress. Programs like Oregon Promise and New York's Excelsior Scholarship represent efforts to implement this model. The Excelsior Scholarship, for instance, has garnered attention for its promise of tuition-free education at public colleges and universities for families earning up to a specified income threshold. However, the program's strict requirements—such as full-time enrollment and residency obligations—often exclude students from the lowest-income brackets who may need to work full-time or support dependents while attending college (Mitchell et al., 2021). Despite these challenges, first-dollar scholarships offer a more comprehensive approach to reducing financial barriers and are particularly beneficial for marginalized populations.

International models further underscore the feasibility of tuition-free education. Germany, for example, has eliminated tuition fees at public universities, allowing students to pursue higher education without the fear of debt accumulation. Advocates in the U.S. argue that adopting similar policies could significantly improve access and equity. However, opponents raise concerns about increased taxation and the potential for over-enrollment, which may strain institutional resources and degrade the quality of education (Goldrick-Rab, 2016).

Reforming the Student Loan System

Student loan debt in the United States has reached alarming levels, with the total debt surpassing $1.7 trillion in 2024 and impacting more than 43 million borrowers (Friedman, 2023). The staggering scale of this debt crisis has profound and far-reaching consequences. It prevents many borrowers from achieving key life milestones such as homeownership, starting families, and building financial stability. For some, it leads to an endless cycle of repayments where the original loan balance remains untouched due to compounding interest, fees, and penalties. The system, initially designed to expand educational access, has instead evolved into a predatory mechanism that traps borrowers in a lifetime of debt.

The Predatory Nature of Student Loans

The predatory nature of the student loan system stems from several factors, including high interest rates, lack of transparency, and policies that disproportionately affect the most vulnerable populations. Federal student loans, often touted as more manageable than private loans, still carry interest rates that frequently outpace inflation. These high rates compound over time, meaning borrowers often repay far more than they originally borrowed. Private loans exacerbate the problem, as they often lack the borrower protections and flexible repayment options that federal loans provide.

Loan servicers also play a significant role in perpetuating the crisis. Companies like Navient, formerly one of the largest federal loan servicers, have been accused of misleading borrowers, pushing them into forbearance instead of income-driven repayment plans, and failing to provide accurate information about repayment options (Consumer Financial Protection Bureau [CFPB], 2022). Such practices result in ballooning balances and years of unnecessary payments, leaving borrowers worse off than when they started.

For many borrowers, the promise of higher education as a pathway to prosperity has become a financial trap. Non-dischargeable in bankruptcy, student loans remain one of the only forms of debt from which individuals cannot escape, even in cases of severe financial hardship. This lack of recourse allows lenders and servicers to continue collecting, even as borrowers struggle to make ends meet. The burden falls disproportionately on marginalized groups, including first-generation college students, minorities, and women, who are more likely to take on higher debt loads and experience lower earnings post-graduation.

Far-Reaching Consequences

The consequences of this predatory system ripple through the broader economy. Young adults burdened with excessive debt are less likely to buy homes, contribute to retirement savings, or invest in their futures. A Federal Reserve report found that student loan debt is a significant factor in delaying homeownership for millennials, with many unable to qualify for mortgages due to their high debt-to-income ratios (Federal Reserve, 2020). Similarly, student debt disproportionately affects borrowers' mental health, with studies showing a strong correlation between high debt levels and anxiety, depression, and even suicidal ideation (Friedman, 2023).

Furthermore, the lifetime earnings premium associated with a college degree is being eroded for many borrowers. While higher education can still provide financial advantages, those advantages are often outweighed by the debt repayments that persist for decades. Some borrowers find themselves in situations where they have repaid the equivalent of their loan principal several times over yet still owe more than the original amount due to compounding interest. This "negative amortization" is particularly common among those enrolled in income-driven repayment plans, where monthly payments often fail to cover interest accrual (Looney & Yannelis, 2020).

Comprehensive Reform: The Way Forward

To address this crisis, comprehensive reform of the student loan system is essential. Policymakers must prioritize three key areas: improving repayment options, expanding loan forgiveness programs, and reducing the overall cost of borrowing.

Improving Repayment Options

Income-driven repayment (IDR) plans, which cap monthly payments at a percentage of discretionary income, have provided relief to some borrowers. However, these plans are often overly complex and difficult to navigate. Simplifying the application process and automatically enrolling borrowers in IDR plans could reduce defaults and make repayment more manageable. Additionally, reducing the repayment period from 20–25 years to 10–15 years would accelerate debt forgiveness and provide tangible relief for millions.

Expanding Loan Forgiveness Programs

Existing forgiveness programs, such as Public Service Loan Forgiveness (PSLF), have been hampered by restrictive eligibility criteria, poor implementation, and administrative inefficiencies. Although PSLF aims to provide loan forgiveness to borrowers working in public service fields such as government, education, healthcare, and nonprofit organizations, the program has been plagued by complex application processes, strict documentation requirements, and high denial rates due to technicalities. As a result, many eligible borrowers have been denied forgiveness despite years of qualifying service, undermining the program's original intent to incentivize careers that serve the public good (Miller et al., 2019).

To make loan forgiveness more effective and equitable, policymakers should consider expanding forgiveness options in several key ways. One approach could be to include private loans in forgiveness programs, which would provide relief to the millions of borrowers who have taken out loans from private lenders, often at higher interest rates and with fewer protections than federal loans. By incorporating private loans into federal forgiveness programs, borrowers would have access to more comprehensive relief and a clearer path toward financial freedom.

Furthermore, there should be a broader push to expand loan forgiveness for low-income borrowers and those from underrepresented communities, who are more likely to carry higher levels of debt and face greater challenges in repaying loans. This could include expanding eligibility for existing forgiveness programs to ensure that more marginalized populations benefit from the relief intended for public service workers.

One innovative approach to loan forgiveness is to allow borrowers to earn forgiveness based on a "service-to-education" ratio. Specifically, for every year of service to the government, military, or any type of service that directly benefits the public, borrowers could receive one year of loan forgiveness for each year they work in a public service role. This would provide clear, direct incentives for individuals to pursue careers that contribute to the public good, such as teaching in underserved areas, working in healthcare facilities, or serving in local government agencies. Not only would this model benefit borrowers, but it would also address critical workforce shortages in sectors that are vital to society's functioning and well-being.

Expanding the scope of loan forgiveness to include such a "service-for-education" model would help ensure that students who enter into public service professions can do so without the looming burden of overwhelming student debt. It also offers a mutually beneficial solution: students can pursue their education with the confidence that their contributions to society will be recognized and rewarded, while governments and public institutions can attract much-needed talent and expertise.

Policymakers should also consider widespread cancellation of a portion of student loan debt, particularly for borrowers with low incomes or those in high-need professions. This could be achieved through a targeted debt cancellation program, which could provide relief to borrowers who have made consistent payments for years but still owe significant amounts due to the capitalized interest and the nature of income-driven repayment plans. Widespread debt forgiveness could be an effective tool in addressing the disproportionate impact of student loan debt on disadvantaged populations, helping to promote economic mobility and reduce wealth inequality.

Ultimately, expanding loan forgiveness options, including service-based forgiveness and targeted debt cancellation, would make the student loan system more equitable and manageable. By rewarding service to the public and ensuring that borrowers in high-need professions can access affordable repayment options, the government can help mitigate the negative impacts of student debt while supporting the vital sectors that underpin the nation's success.

Reducing the Cost of Borrowing

Interest rates on federal student loans should be lowered to match inflation, ensuring that borrowers are not penalized for seeking an education. For those already burdened by high-interest loans, refinancing options at lower rates should be made widely available. Additionally, placing stricter regulations on private lenders would help curb predatory practices and provide borrowers with more equitable options.

The student loan crisis in America is not merely a financial problem; it is a moral and social challenge that reflects the systemic inequities within higher education. Without meaningful reform, millions of borrowers will remain trapped in cycles of debt that limit their potential and perpetuate inequality. Addressing this issue requires a comprehensive rethinking of the student loan system, prioritizing borrower protections, equitable access to education, and sustainable repayment structures. Only by transforming the system can we ensure that education fulfills its promise as a pathway to opportunity, not a lifetime of financial servitude.

Income-Driven Repayment Plans

Income-driven repayment (IDR) plans are designed to make loan payments more manageable by capping them at a percentage of borrowers' discretionary income. While these plans have provided relief to some borrowers, their complexity has hindered broader adoption. Many borrowers are unaware of their eligibility or struggle to navigate the application process, resulting in low enrollment rates (Looney & Yannelis, 2020). Simplifying these plans, streamlining enrollment, and increasing outreach efforts could enhance their effectiveness. Moreover, automatically enrolling borrowers in IDR plans at the time of loan disbursement could significantly reduce default rates and ensure that repayment remains affordable throughout borrowers' careers.

In addition to improving access, proposals have called for modifying IDR plans to include shorter repayment terms and broader eligibility criteria. For instance, reducing the repayment term from 20–25 years to 10–15 years could accelerate debt forgiveness and alleviate long-term financial stress for borrowers. Expanding eligibility to include Parent PLUS loans and private loans could also provide relief to a wider range of borrowers.

Loan Forgiveness Programs

Loan forgiveness programs, such as Public Service Loan Forgiveness (PSLF), aim to incentivize careers in public service fields, including education, healthcare, and law enforcement. Despite their noble intentions, these programs have faced significant criticism for their restrictive eligibility requirements and poor implementation. A 2019 report found that over 99% of PSLF applications were denied due to technicalities or incomplete paperwork (Miller et al., 2019). To address these issues, policymakers have proposed expanding forgiveness options, simplifying the application process, and increasing funding for program administration. Broader reforms, such as automatic enrollment in forgiveness programs for qualifying borrowers, could further enhance participation rates and ensure that the intended benefits reach those who need them most.

Interest Rate Reductions

High interest rates on federal student loans have become one of the most significant contributors to the growing student debt crisis in the United States. The compounded interest on loans can quickly balloon the total amount owed, sometimes more than doubling the original debt amount. This becomes particularly burdensome for borrowers in income-driven repayment plans, where monthly payments often only cover the interest, not the principal balance, leading to a situation where many borrowers are paying for years or even decades without ever reducing the original loan amount. For example, borrowers who take out large loans for graduate or professional degrees often find themselves paying back more in interest than the amount they borrowed. This issue is exacerbated by the fact that federal loans carry fixed interest rates that are higher than other forms of borrowing, and these rates are determined by legislation, not by market conditions (Dynarski et al., 2018).

Proposals to reduce or even eliminate interest on federal student loans have gained traction as a potential solution to this problem. Reducing or eliminating interest would allow borrowers to focus on paying down the principal of their loans rather than getting caught in a cycle of debt that perpetuates over time. Such a reform could bring immediate relief to borrowers, particularly those who are struggling financially or working in low-paying jobs, by decreasing the overall financial burden. For example, borrowers with a lower income would be able to allocate more of their monthly payments toward the principal balance, rather than paying off interest fees that continue to accumulate despite their efforts.

However, there are concerns that reducing interest rates may disproportionately benefit higher-income borrowers, particularly those who borrow large sums for graduate or professional programs, which tend to offer higher salaries after graduation. Critics argue that these borrowers, who may not face the same financial struggles as low-income students, would benefit more from an interest rate reduction than those who are struggling with smaller loans from undergraduate studies (Dynarski et al., 2018). To ensure that the policy benefits are distributed equitably, policymakers could consider targeted interest rate reductions. These targeted reductions would prioritize borrowers with lower incomes, those working in critical fields such as teaching, healthcare, and social services, or borrowers in income-driven repayment plans. This approach could ensure that the reform addresses the needs of those most affected by the student debt crisis, while still providing relief to a broader swath of borrowers.

Holding Colleges Accountable for Financial Transparency and Outcomes

Colleges and universities play a central role in shaping the affordability and value of higher education, yet they often lack sufficient accountability regarding tuition costs and student outcomes. In many cases, tuition continues to rise while institutional spending, especially on administrative costs, has skyrocketed. Despite the increasing financial burdens placed on students and families, many schools fail to demonstrate measurable improvements in student success, including graduation rates, post-graduation employment, and long-term financial outcomes. Holding institutions accountable for these outcomes is essential in addressing the broader issue of affordability and ensuring that higher education remains a sound investment for all students.

Accountability can take various forms, but one of the most effective measures is requiring colleges and universities to disclose clear, detailed financial information. This transparency would allow students and families to make more informed decisions about where they invest their time and money. It would also put pressure on institutions to align their financial priorities with their educational goals. For example, if an institution is spending a significant portion of its budget on lavish amenities or expanding administrative staff at the expense of teaching and student support services, this would be clearly reflected in its financial reporting. Institutions should also be required to disclose information about their outcomes, such as graduation rates, job placement rates, average starting salaries, and student loan repayment rates. By linking funding to these measurable outcomes, schools would have an incentive to prioritize student success over increasing tuition and expanding administrative functions.

Increased accountability also means implementing systems for institutional assessment that go beyond graduation rates alone. Colleges and universities should be required to demonstrate that their programs are aligned with the needs of the workforce and that graduates are not only receiving a degree but also acquiring the skills necessary to succeed in the labor market. This could include increasing partnerships between higher education institutions and industries to create curriculum that better prepares students for careers in high-demand fields. Institutions that fail to meet performance benchmarks should face consequences, such as a reduction in state or federal funding or limitations on student loan eligibility for their programs.

Transparency in Tuition and Fees

One of the greatest challenges prospective students face is navigating the true cost of attending college. Tuition, fees, and other expenses—such as books, room, board, and transportation—are often presented as a single, unified figure, obscuring the full financial burden students will face. This lack of transparency makes it difficult for students and families to accurately assess the affordability of their college options and compare costs between institutions. As a result, many students take on debt without fully understanding the financial impact, and some are caught off guard by hidden fees or unanticipated costs that add thousands of dollars to their financial obligations.

To address this issue, policymakers should mandate standardized reporting of tuition and fees across all institutions of higher learning. This reporting should go beyond just listing tuition rates and include a detailed breakdown of all fees associated with enrollment, including administrative fees, technology fees, student activity fees, and campus-related charges. Additionally, colleges should be required to provide estimates for the full cost of attendance, including housing, food, transportation, and other living expenses, so that students can better understand the financial commitments they are making. By making these costs more transparent, prospective students can make more informed decisions about where to attend college and avoid being caught off guard by unexpected expenses.

Tools like net price calculators, which allow students to estimate their out-of-pocket costs based on family income, financial aid eligibility, and other factors, can also provide a clearer picture of the true cost of education. Mandating that all institutions have an easy-to-use, accessible net price calculator would help prospective students better plan their finances and avoid taking on debt they cannot afford. Moreover, the inclusion of these tools could foster healthy competition between schools, encouraging them to lower tuition rates and reduce unnecessary fees in order to remain competitive in the marketplace.

Performance-Based Funding

Performance-based funding (PBF) is a funding model that ties a portion of public funding to measurable outcomes, such as graduation rates, job placement statistics, and student loan repayment rates. The idea behind this model is to incentivize colleges and universities to focus on improving student outcomes and ensuring that their graduates are well-equipped for the workforce. By linking funding to these outcomes, institutions would have a financial stake in ensuring that students not only graduate but do so with the skills and qualifications needed to succeed in their careers. This approach could help address the growing concern that many students are graduating with degrees that do not translate into gainful employment or a high return on investment.

However, critics of performance-based funding caution that it may lead to unintended consequences. For example, institutions may be incentivized to enroll fewer students from disadvantaged backgrounds or to "weed out" students who are at risk of not graduating in order to maintain high graduation rates. This could exacerbate existing inequities and make it even harder for underrepresented populations to access higher education (Dougherty & Reddy, 2013). To mitigate these risks, performance-based funding models should be designed with equity in mind. This means that metrics should account for the demographics of the student population, and funding should be adjusted to reflect the challenges faced by schools that serve large numbers of low-income or first-generation college students.

Furthermore, the metrics used in performance-based funding should go beyond simple graduation rates. While graduation rates are important, they do not capture the full range of student success. For example, students who attend school part-time or who take longer to graduate may still be successful in terms of career outcomes and earnings. Additionally, metrics should include measures of post-graduation employment, job placement in high-wage fields, and student loan repayment rates. By focusing on a broader range of outcomes, performance-based funding can encourage schools to invest in programs and strategies that help students succeed both in the classroom and in the workforce, ensuring that the model promotes equitable access to education and supports long-term economic mobility.

Caps on Administrative Spending

Over the past two decades, the rise in administrative spending at colleges and universities has become a significant concern, particularly as these costs often outpace investments in academic programs and student services. The rapid expansion of administrative functions—such as increased staff for compliance, diversity initiatives, marketing, and student affairs—has contributed to an overall increase in the cost of higher education. As a result, tuition fees have risen to cover these expenses, putting a greater financial strain on students and their families. In fact, studies have shown that administrative costs in higher education have grown at a much faster rate than instructional costs, with administrative staff now outnumbering faculty in many institutions (Ehrenberg, 2012).

Critics argue that these expenditures are not always aligned with the core mission of educational institutions, which is to provide quality instruction and support for student success. Instead, many universities have prioritized building lavish campuses, expanding non-academic services, and increasing administrative layers. While some of these administrative positions may be important, such as those focused on compliance with federal regulations or student services, others are viewed as unnecessary and disproportionately large compared to the needs of the student body. As a result, the growing cost of administration is often seen as a major contributor to the overall rise in tuition, with limited returns for the students paying those higher fees.

One potential solution to this issue is the implementation of caps on administrative spending, which would require institutions to limit the percentage of their budgets allocated to administrative costs. By setting clear spending guidelines, colleges could redirect funds toward more critical areas, such as academic programs, faculty salaries, student support services, and research. This shift would ensure that tuition dollars are primarily spent on the educational experiences and resources that directly benefit students. For instance, institutions could reduce spending on non-essential services or high-cost administrative projects and instead focus on improving teaching quality, expanding academic offerings, or increasing access to mental health resources for students.

Additionally, policymakers could incentivize cost-sharing measures, such as consolidating administrative functions across campuses or systems, particularly for public universities or multi-campus institutions. Many universities have duplicative administrative functions that could be streamlined or centralized, reducing the overall overhead expenses. For example, large university systems with multiple campuses could consolidate human resources, marketing, or IT departments, thereby cutting down on the need for separate administrative offices for each campus. Such collaborations could lead to significant savings and allow universities to reinvest those funds into enhancing the educational experience for students.

The primary goal of these reforms is to ensure that financial resources are being used efficiently and effectively. By holding institutions accountable for their administrative spending, it would be possible to ensure that universities are prioritizing their core mission of educating students while also addressing the rising costs that make higher education increasingly unaffordable.

Debt-to-Earnings Ratios

One of the most significant challenges in addressing the affordability of higher education is ensuring that the investment in a degree results in a return that justifies the financial burden. For many students, the promise of a college degree is a pathway to economic mobility and higher earnings. However, for some degree programs, particularly those in low-paying fields, the debt-to-earnings ratio—a measure of how much debt graduates incur relative to their post-graduation earnings—can be shockingly high. This raises critical questions about the value of certain degrees and whether students are receiving a fair return on their investment.

Requiring colleges and universities to report debt-to-earnings ratios for graduates in specific programs would provide students and prospective enrollees with valuable information to make more informed decisions about their education. This metric would help reveal how much debt students from particular programs are carrying after graduation and whether they are able to earn enough in their chosen field to pay off that debt in a reasonable time frame. For example, graduates of high-cost programs in the humanities or the arts may face a situation where their earnings post-graduation are insufficient to cover their student loan obligations. In contrast, graduates from highly specialized technical fields, like computer science or engineering, often enjoy higher starting salaries, making it easier to repay loans in a timely manner.

By requiring institutions to publicly report these ratios, students would have more transparency about the financial outcomes of their degree choices. This would also incentivize universities to ensure that their programs are designed to provide students with skills that are in demand in the labor market and that offer competitive salaries. Institutions with consistently poor debt-to-earnings ratios in certain programs could face penalties or lose eligibility for federal financial aid, encouraging them to prioritize the financial viability and value of the degrees they offer. For instance, if a program consistently produces graduates who are unable to pay off their student loans or struggle with significant debt, the institution might be incentivized to either improve the program's quality, adjust its costs, or even discontinue it in favor of more viable alternatives.

Creating a publicly accessible database of debt-to-earnings ratios for graduates by program would empower prospective students to choose programs that align with their financial and career goals. This information could be made available on college and university websites or through independent platforms that aggregate this data, making it easy for students to compare potential earnings against the costs of various degrees. Armed with this knowledge, students could make more strategic decisions about their education, minimizing the risk of taking on excessive debt for degrees that do not lead to lucrative career opportunities.

This data could also help policymakers ensure that federal financial aid is being used effectively. Currently, federal student loans are available for a wide range of degree programs, including those with low earning potential. By linking loan eligibility to debt-to-earnings ratios, it may be possible to guide federal funding toward programs that have higher rates of return for students, ensuring that taxpayer money is being invested in fields that provide the most economic benefit to graduates and society. In the long run, this type of transparency and accountability could help reduce the student loan burden while improving the value of higher education for all students.

Chapter 15

A Call to Action: Saving Higher Education

Higher education stands at a crossroads, burdened by escalating costs, growing student debt, and an increasing disconnect between academic outcomes and the needs of the workforce. The promise of education as a pathway to opportunity and social mobility is being undermined, leaving millions of students and families to bear the weight of an outdated system. In this chapter, we call for a collective effort—one that bridges the gap between governments, private sectors, and educational institutions, and that empowers students, alumni, and faculty to advocate for meaningful change. It is time to reinvent higher education, not just as a means of earning a degree, but as a powerful tool for equity, opportunity, and societal progress. Through collaboration, transparency, and a renewed focus on accessibility, we can reshape the future of higher education to serve all students and society at large.

Encouraging Collaboration Between Governments, Private Sectors, and Institutions

The crisis in higher education affordability and access is one of the most pressing challenges of our time, and it requires a comprehensive, multifaceted approach to resolve. For decades, the rising cost of education, coupled with stagnant wages and increasing student debt, has placed a heavy burden on students and their families. This crisis is not merely a financial issue but a societal one, impacting the workforce, economic mobility, and even national competitiveness in a rapidly changing global economy. To address this crisis, a true collaboration between governments, the private sector, and higher education institutions is imperative. Each of these stakeholders has unique strengths and responsibilities, and by working together, they can create a more sustainable, equitable, and responsive higher education system.

Government's Role in Higher Education Reform

The government plays a foundational role in shaping the higher education landscape, not just through funding but also through policy and regulation. Governments at both the federal and state levels must prioritize higher education, ensuring that it remains accessible and affordable for all students, regardless of their socioeconomic background. One of the first steps is increasing funding for public colleges and universities, which serve the majority of students from low- and middle-income families. Governments should recognize that the long-term benefits of investing in education—ranging from a more skilled workforce to a stronger economy—far outweigh the costs.

However, simply increasing funding is not enough. Public investments must be tied to performance and outcomes to ensure that they are used effectively. Governments can implement performance-based funding models, where financial support for institutions is linked to tangible results such as graduation rates, job placement, and student success. This system would encourage institutions to prioritize student retention, career readiness, and support services. Furthermore, policies that foster transparency in pricing and outcomes—requiring universities to publish clear information about tuition, fees, and the return on investment for graduates—would empower students and families to make more informed decisions about where to pursue higher education (Dougherty & Reddy, 2013).

Governments also have a role in creating alternative pathways to education, especially for nontraditional students. These could include increasing support for community colleges, trade schools, and vocational programs, which are critical to meeting the diverse needs of the workforce. Such programs can provide valuable skills and certifications without the burdens of a traditional four-year degree, which is not always necessary for certain high-demand occupations. Additionally, government policies should encourage partnerships with industry to ensure that education aligns with workforce needs, ensuring that graduates are prepared for the evolving job market.

Private Sector's Role in Higher Education Reform

The private sector, including businesses, foundations, and nonprofit organizations, must also play an integral role in reforming higher education. Businesses across various industries are deeply invested in the skills and qualifications of the future workforce, and they can no longer afford to be passive observers of the education system. Private sector companies should partner with higher education institutions to align curriculum with industry needs. This collaboration could include co-developing specialized programs, internships, apprenticeships, and mentorships that provide students with the real-world experience necessary to thrive in their careers.

Moreover, businesses can offer financial support through scholarships, grants, and research partnerships. Companies like Google, Microsoft, and Amazon have already begun investing in alternative education models, such as coding boot camps and industry-specific certification programs, which provide a quicker, more affordable route to employable skills. These initiatives can complement traditional degree programs, offering students a diverse range of options to gain marketable skills. By participating in the funding of such programs, private corporations can help increase access to education for underserved populations while ensuring that they have access to a skilled workforce that meets their needs (Kelchen, 2021).

In addition to direct educational investments, the private sector can advocate for systemic changes that support higher education reform. Businesses that have a stake in the quality and diversity of the workforce can use their influence to lobby for changes in education policy that address issues such as tuition inflation, student debt, and workforce preparation. Corporate social responsibility (CSR) programs can also be leveraged to fund initiatives that support underrepresented students, particularly those in high-need fields. Through these efforts, the private sector can not only help alleviate financial barriers to education but also ensure a more equitable distribution of opportunity.

The Role of Higher Education Institutions in Reform

Higher education institutions themselves must take a proactive role in addressing the affordability crisis and ensuring that they are preparing students for the future. Universities and colleges need to reassess their priorities and spending, particularly in light of rising tuition fees. Too often, the increase in tuition is not accompanied by proportional improvements in academic services or student outcomes. Administrative costs, especially those unrelated to direct student support, have ballooned over the years, diverting funds away from the core educational mission. By implementing caps on administrative spending and focusing resources on improving teaching quality and student support, institutions can make education more affordable without sacrificing quality (Ehrenberg, 2012).

Colleges must also embrace innovative educational models that can reduce costs and increase access. For example, competency-based education allows students to progress based on their mastery of skills rather than the amount of time spent in class. This can make learning more personalized and efficient, particularly for adult learners or those balancing work and study. Similarly, institutions must continue to invest in online learning, which has proven to be a cost-effective way to deliver quality education to a broader audience. By creating partnerships with businesses to offer certifications or stackable credentials, institutions can also provide students with alternative pathways to career readiness that do not require a traditional four-year degree.

172

Finally, universities should engage more deeply with the communities they serve. This means not only offering education but also collaborating with local governments, nonprofits, and industries to address regional needs. Universities can serve as hubs of innovation, research, and problem-solving, working alongside local businesses to develop solutions to societal challenges. For example, universities could partner with cities to develop sustainable urban planning strategies, or with hospitals to advance medical research that directly benefits public health. By connecting educational efforts to real-world applications, institutions can strengthen their relevance and impact while ensuring that students graduate with the skills and knowledge necessary to meet the challenges of the future.

A Shared Responsibility for Education Reform

The reform of higher education cannot be the responsibility of any one sector alone. Governments, private industries, and educational institutions must come together to create a comprehensive, sustainable approach to education reform. By collaborating, sharing resources, and aligning priorities, these stakeholders can help build a system of higher education that is more equitable, affordable, and aligned with the needs of the modern workforce. This collaborative approach will not only improve access to higher education but also ensure that it serves as a tool for economic mobility, societal progress, and long-term national competitiveness.

Government's Role in Higher Education Reform

The government plays an indispensable role in shaping the future of higher education in the United States. As the primary body responsible for funding, policy development, and regulation, the government must work to create a more accessible, affordable, and equitable system of higher education. A key aspect of this is ensuring that public institutions, particularly community colleges and state universities, are adequately funded, as these institutions serve the majority of students from low- and middle-income families. By prioritizing investments in these institutions, the government can help provide a broader range of students with the opportunity to pursue higher education and ultimately increase the nation's level of educational attainment, which in turn can contribute to economic growth and social mobility.

Increasing Funding and Tying Resources to Outcomes

A primary responsibility of the government is to allocate sufficient funds to public universities and community colleges to ensure they can operate effectively and meet the demands of an increasingly diverse student body. However, merely increasing funding is not enough; the government must also ensure that these funds are used effectively and lead to tangible improvements in educational outcomes. One way to accomplish this is by tying funding to performance metrics, such as student success, graduation rates, and post-graduation employment. Performance-based funding models, where institutions receive funding based on their ability to help students succeed, are gaining traction as a way to align financial support with outcomes (Dougherty & Reddy, 2013).

Such models reward institutions that demonstrate consistent improvements in student retention, graduation, and placement in high-paying, sustainable jobs. This would encourage universities to prioritize student services, provide strong career counseling, and increase engagement with employers to ensure that students are gaining the skills that are in demand in the workforce. Moreover, such a system would help reduce the reliance on simplistic measures like enrollment numbers, which do not necessarily correlate with student success or long-term outcomes.

In addition to directly funding public institutions, the government can provide tax incentives for private institutions that align with public goals, such as improving access to education, affordability, and workforce readiness. For example, private colleges and universities that develop programs targeted at underserved populations or create affordable pathways to degree completion could be rewarded with tax breaks or other financial incentives. Encouraging these institutions to focus on producing outcomes that benefit society—such as graduates who are prepared for critical workforce needs—can help bridge the growing gap between the skills students are taught and the skills employers require (Kelchen, 2021).

Fostering Innovation through Policy Reform

Beyond funding, government policy must also foster innovation and the continuous evolution of higher education to keep pace with the changing needs of society. Traditional models of education, which have been built around four-year degree programs, are increasingly being viewed as insufficient for addressing the diverse needs of students and the labor market. Today's students need educational opportunities that are flexible, affordable, and responsive to the dynamic nature of work, especially as industries evolve and new technologies emerge.

Governments must encourage policies that promote educational innovation, such as the development of alternative pathways to degree attainment. Industry-recognized certifications, credentials, and apprenticeships can provide students with valuable skills that complement traditional degree programs. These programs are typically shorter, more affordable, and more directly tied to job-specific competencies, making them an attractive option for many students. For example, in fields like technology, healthcare, and skilled trades, certifications or apprenticeships can often lead to high-paying jobs that don't require a four-year degree (Kelchen, 2021). By incentivizing the creation and expansion of these alternative pathways, the government can help broaden access to higher education and make the transition from school to the workforce smoother and more accessible.

Moreover, government policy should encourage the use of technology to improve educational delivery. The rise of online education has the potential to provide greater access to education for nontraditional students, including working adults, students from rural areas, and those with caregiving responsibilities. Policymakers can work to ensure that online education maintains rigorous standards and that students have access to the necessary resources and support to succeed. For example, ensuring equitable access to high-speed internet, providing funding for online course development, and supporting faculty training for online teaching are critical components of improving the accessibility and quality of digital education.

Prioritizing Financial Transparency and Accountability

Financial transparency and accountability are central to ensuring that higher education remains accessible and affordable. The government must mandate that institutions clearly disclose essential financial data, such as tuition costs, fees, and total cost of attendance, so that students and families can make more informed decisions about their education. Currently, the complexity and opacity of tuition pricing make it difficult for prospective students to understand the true cost of attending college, leading many to take on more debt than they initially anticipate. Requiring institutions to provide clear breakdowns of tuition, fees, and other costs—along with data on student loan default rates, employment outcomes, and income post-graduation—would enable students to evaluate the return on investment for different programs and institutions (Dougherty & Reddy, 2013).

Additionally, the government must hold institutions accountable for their financial management, ensuring that funds are being allocated in ways that maximize student success. This can be done through regular audits, performance reviews, and requiring schools to justify tuition increases. Institutions should be required to prove that any increase in tuition directly correlates with improvements in educational quality, student services, or workforce alignment. This would ensure that the money students invest in their education is being used effectively and not simply contributing to rising administrative costs or institutional profits.

Creating Pathways to Workforce Readiness

Government efforts should also prioritize the development of policies that align higher education with workforce needs. This includes incentivizing the creation of programs that provide students with the

176

skills necessary to succeed in fast-growing sectors like technology, green energy, and healthcare. Partnerships between universities, community colleges, and industries can be particularly effective in creating job-focused programs that provide students with both theoretical knowledge and hands-on experience. By collaborating with businesses and employers, educational institutions can develop curricula that meet the needs of the workforce while providing students with clear career paths.

Furthermore, governments can support workforce development initiatives by providing funding to institutions that create partnerships with employers to offer work-based learning opportunities, such as internships, co-op programs, and apprenticeships. These initiatives ensure that students gain practical experience while still in school, giving them a competitive advantage in the job market upon graduation. For students, these opportunities provide not only valuable work experience, but also potential job offers and higher employment rates after graduation.

In sum, the government's role in higher education reform is multifaceted and essential to the creation of an accessible, affordable, and equitable educational system. By prioritizing funding for public institutions, encouraging innovation through alternative pathways, demanding financial transparency, and creating strong connections between education and the workforce, the government can help shape a higher education system that meets the needs of today's students and the demands of the modern economy. Only through such comprehensive reforms can the promise of higher education as a tool for upward mobility, social equity, and economic progress be fully realized.

Private Sector's Role in Higher Education

The private sector has an increasingly vital role to play in the reform of higher education, especially as the landscape of work and education rapidly changes. Businesses, non-profit organizations, and philanthropic entities are uniquely positioned to collaborate with educational institutions to help bridge the growing skills gap and ensure that students are equipped with the knowledge and experience necessary for success in the modern workforce. The private sector, with its wealth of resources, expertise, and innovation, can drive change in higher education by fostering partnerships, investing in workforce development, and providing financial and experiential support to students.

Collaborative Curriculum Development

One of the key contributions the private sector can make to higher education reform is in the area of curriculum development. The pace of technological change, coupled with globalization, has created an evolving job market where the skills needed for success are constantly shifting. Educational institutions often struggle to keep pace with these changes, leading to a disconnect between what students are taught and the skills employers need. Private sector companies, particularly in industries such as technology, healthcare, and manufacturing, can collaborate with higher education institutions to design curricula that are responsive to these shifts.

For example, companies like Microsoft, Google, and IBM have already initiated partnerships with universities to develop courses and programs that focus on high-demand skills such as coding, data analytics, and artificial intelligence. By working closely with educators, businesses can ensure that the curriculum remains relevant, up-to-date, and focused on the competencies that students need to succeed. These partnerships also allow businesses to have input into the development of programs that can lead to better job preparation for students and a stronger connection between higher education and the workforce. Ultimately, this collaboration helps ensure that graduates are not only academically qualified but also job-ready upon completion of their studies (Kelchen, 2021).

Internships, Apprenticeships, and Co-op Programs

In addition to helping shape the curriculum, the private sector can play a pivotal role in providing students with hands-on, real-world experiences that are critical for workforce readiness. Internships, apprenticeships, and co-op programs are essential tools for bridging the gap between classroom learning and the practical demands of the job market. Through these partnerships, businesses can provide students with the opportunity to gain industry-specific knowledge and skills while still in school, making them more competitive candidates when they graduate.

Private-sector companies can offer paid internships that not only give students valuable work experience but also help offset the costs of their education. These programs provide a dual benefit: students acquire essential workplace skills, and employers gain access to a pool of talented, educated individuals who are already familiar with their company's operations and culture. Additionally, these experiences often lead to job offers after graduation, creating a seamless transition from education to employment. For example, healthcare companies can partner with nursing schools to provide clinical placements for nursing students, while tech companies can offer software development internships for computer science students. These hands-on learning opportunities ensure that students are not just learning theory but also applying their knowledge in a real-world context, making them better prepared for the demands of their careers (Dougherty & Reddy, 2013).

Private-Sector Financial Investments

The private sector's involvement in higher education reform extends beyond curriculum and internships; it also includes direct financial investments that can help alleviate the rising costs of education. As tuition fees increase, private companies, philanthropic foundations, and alumni groups have an important role to play in making higher education more accessible, particularly for underrepresented and low-income students. These groups can provide scholarships, grants, and loan repayment assistance that directly support students in need.

Philanthropic organizations, such as the Bill & Melinda Gates Foundation, have already made significant contributions to improving college access for underserved communities through initiatives like the Gates Millennium Scholars Program, which has helped thousands of students from low-income families attend college. Similarly, corporations with a vested interest in workforce development can create scholarship programs specifically targeted at students pursuing degrees in high-demand fields such as STEM (Science, Technology, Engineering, and Mathematics). These financial contributions not only make higher education more accessible but also help reduce the burden of student loan debt, which has become a significant financial challenge for many graduates.

In addition to scholarships and financial aid, the private sector can contribute to career development and job readiness by providing mentorship opportunities, internships, and networking platforms that connect students with industry leaders. These programs can be designed to match students with professionals in their fields of study, giving them the chance to gain insights into the industry, receive career advice, and build relationships that can lead to job opportunities after graduation.

Business-Supported Research and Development

The private sector can also support higher education by funding research and development projects that address societal challenges and advance knowledge in key areas. Universities are critical hubs for innovation, but they often lack the financial resources to fully support the scale of research needed to make meaningful advancements. Private sector investments in research can help address this gap, especially when the research is aligned with both academic goals and industry needs. For instance, tech companies may fund university-led projects focused on artificial intelligence or cybersecurity, while healthcare companies could sponsor medical research aimed at finding new treatments or technologies.

These collaborations can also facilitate the transfer of knowledge between academia and industry, allowing for the commercialization of academic discoveries and innovations. By funding research initiatives, private companies not only contribute to the advancement of knowledge but also ensure that the work being done in universities is relevant to the market and addresses the real-world problems that businesses and society face. This, in turn, creates a mutually beneficial environment where universities gain the resources and support to conduct cutting-edge research, and businesses gain access to the latest innovations and highly skilled graduates ready to implement them.

Mentorship, Career Development, and Networking

In addition to providing financial support and practical experience, the private sector can also play an instrumental role in shaping students' careers through mentorship and networking opportunities. Many students, especially those from underrepresented backgrounds, may lack access to the professional networks and mentorship that are critical for career advancement. Through initiatives like mentorship programs, career development workshops, and networking events, private companies can help level the playing field and provide students with the tools and connections they need to succeed.

For instance, companies could partner with universities to offer mentorship opportunities where students are paired with professionals who can offer guidance, career advice, and support throughout their academic journey. These mentorship relationships can help students build confidence, gain industry insights, and navigate the complexities of launching a career. Additionally, career fairs and networking events organized by businesses can connect students with potential employers, offering direct pathways to internships, job placements, and career opportunities that might not otherwise be accessible.

The private sector's contributions to higher education reform are essential in ensuring that educational outcomes align with workforce needs and that students are prepared for success in a rapidly changing global economy. By collaborating with universities to develop relevant curricula, offering real-world experiences through internships and apprenticeships, providing financial investments such as scholarships and grants, and supporting research and career development, businesses can help create a more equitable and effective higher education system. Ultimately, these efforts benefit both the students who gain access to quality education and the industries that gain a highly skilled, well-prepared workforce ready to meet the challenges of the future.

Institutions as the Cornerstone of Reform

Higher education institutions themselves must take a proactive role in reforming the system. For too long, universities and colleges have largely reacted to external pressures rather than driving their own transformation. To meet the evolving needs of students and the workforce, institutions must embrace a fundamental rethinking of how they operate, how they allocate resources, and how they structure their academic programs. At the core of this reform is the need for institutions to offer education that is not only affordable but also relevant to the demands of today's workforce. With the cost of higher education continuing to rise, it is more important than ever for universities to provide students with value—a strong education that equips them with the skills necessary to succeed in a competitive global economy.

Reassessing Tuition Structures and Resource Allocation

One critical area that institutions must address is tuition pricing. Over the past several decades, tuition has risen significantly, outpacing inflation and placing a substantial financial burden on students and families. Institutions must reassess their tuition structures to ensure that they reflect the true cost of education while also maintaining affordability. This includes evaluating the return on investment for students—ensuring that the cost of education is justified by the skills and opportunities it provides. Universities should look for innovative ways to lower tuition costs without sacrificing quality. This could involve streamlining operations, reducing unnecessary administrative expenditures, or cutting back on non-essential programs and services that do not directly contribute to student success.

Alongside reevaluating tuition costs, institutions must also reassess how they allocate their financial resources. Too often, a significant portion of institutional budgets is directed toward administrative functions and non-academic services, leaving less for teaching, faculty salaries, and student support programs. Universities should focus on directing a greater share of their resources toward improving instructional quality and supporting student success. This could include investing in faculty development, expanding academic advising services, improving mental health and wellness resources, and providing career counseling to better prepare students for life after graduation (Ehrenberg, 2012). Moreover, reducing administrative costs—such as scaling back on high-salaried administrative positions or consolidating functions across campuses—could help institutions direct more funding toward academics and student services.

Fostering a Culture of Innovation and Collaboration

Institutions must also foster a culture of innovation that extends beyond the classroom. As the needs of students and employers evolve, universities must be flexible and forward-thinking in how they deliver education. This involves embracing new educational models that allow for more personalized, flexible learning experiences. Competency-based education (CBE) is one such model that holds great promise. CBE allows students to progress at their own pace, earning credit based on the mastery of skills and competencies rather than the number of hours spent in class. This approach enables students to learn in a way that is more suited to their individual learning styles, giving them the flexibility to accelerate their studies or take more time when necessary (Kelchen, 2021).

Moreover, institutions should be more open to collaborating with government agencies and private companies to address pressing societal challenges. Universities have long been centers of research and innovation, but in today's fast-paced world, they must find ways to translate academic research into tangible solutions to global problems. By fostering collaboration between academia, government, and the private sector, universities can drive research that addresses urgent issues such as climate change, public health, and technological advancements. These collaborations can also help students gain exposure to real-world challenges, equipping them with the skills necessary to tackle complex problems after graduation.

Institutions should also work closely with local communities to ensure that their academic offerings align with regional needs. Universities must be more involved in workforce development, particularly in areas where there is a shortage of skilled workers. This can be achieved by offering programs that target industries with high demand for labor, such as healthcare, technology, and renewable energy. By tailoring educational offerings to local economic needs, universities can ensure that students are prepared for successful careers that contribute to the local economy, while also addressing national and global workforce demands.

Building a Sustainable Framework for Reform

Higher education reform cannot occur in isolation. It requires a collaborative effort across multiple sectors, including government, private industry, and educational institutions. Together, these sectors must create a framework for reform that promotes long-term sustainability, equity, and access to higher education. This comprehensive approach will help ensure that students are equipped with the skills they need to succeed in the future workforce and that institutions remain relevant and responsive to the changing needs of society. Only through meaningful collaboration can the nation build a higher education system that prepares students for success in a rapidly changing global economy.

Role of Alumni, Students, and Faculty in Pushing for Reform

While the involvement of governments, private corporations, and educational institutions is crucial to the transformation of higher education, the active participation of alumni, students, and faculty is just as essential. These groups have firsthand experience with the challenges that higher education faces, and their voices and actions are indispensable in driving the momentum for meaningful reform. Alumni, students, and faculty can be powerful advocates for change, helping to shape the policies, programs, and structures that impact students' educational experiences.

Alumni as Catalysts for Change

Alumni play a particularly important role in advocating for change. As former students who have navigated the current educational system, they are uniquely positioned to reflect on the value of their education and its relevance to the real world. Alumni can serve as powerful advocates for reform by sharing their experiences, both positive and negative, with current students, faculty, administrators, and policymakers. For example, alumni who have faced significant financial challenges or who are burdened with high levels of student debt can advocate for more affordable tuition pricing or changes to student loan policies.

Moreover, alumni can use their influence to lobby for institutional policies that better align academic programs with workforce demands. By engaging in discussions with university administrators and policymakers, alumni can help ensure that curricula reflect current trends in the labor market and that students are prepared for high-demand careers. Alumni can also advocate for improvements in career services, networking opportunities, and job placement programs that help graduates transition successfully into the workforce.

Engaging in Fundraising and Financial Support

Alumni can also contribute to higher education reform through financial support. Many universities face significant funding gaps, particularly when it comes to supporting underrepresented students. Alumni can engage in fundraising efforts that promote access and affordability, contributing to scholarships, grants, and loan repayment assistance programs. By giving back to their alma mater, alumni help ensure that future generations of students can access the same opportunities that they did, without facing crippling debt or financial barriers.

In addition to traditional financial donations, alumni can also support initiatives that promote diversity, equity, and inclusion within higher education. By funding outreach programs, mentorship initiatives, or diversity scholarships, alumni can help create a more inclusive academic environment and ensure that students from all backgrounds have the opportunity to succeed.

Students as Advocates for Change

Students, as the primary beneficiaries of higher education, must be active participants in advocating for reform. Through student organizations, petitions, and campaigns, students can raise awareness about issues such as tuition inflation, campus resources, mental health services, and the quality of instruction. Students have the power to mobilize and push for policy changes that directly impact their educational experience. For example, students can work with university administrators to advocate for more affordable textbook options, expanded mental health services, or improved career development programs.

Students can also participate in collaborative efforts with faculty to ensure that academic programs remain relevant to their needs and future careers. By organizing focus groups, surveys, or town hall meetings, students can provide valuable input into program development and help shape the curriculum to better align with both academic and professional aspirations.

Faculty as Leaders in Educational Reform

Faculty members are central to the mission of higher education. They shape the learning experience, contribute to research, and provide mentorship and guidance to students. Faculty must take an active role in advocating for reforms that improve both the quality of education and the affordability of higher education. This could involve supporting new teaching methods, such as competency-based education or experiential learning, that cater to diverse learning styles and help students gain real-world skills.

Faculty also have an important role to play in the governance of their institutions. By participating in faculty committees, holding leadership positions, and collaborating with administrators, faculty members can ensure that institutional policies reflect the needs and interests of students. Faculty can also work with alumni and students to push for changes that align the institution's mission with societal and workforce needs.

In sum, alumni, students, and faculty must collaborate to create a movement for reform that focuses on improving the quality, accessibility, and affordability of higher education. By amplifying their voices and engaging in proactive advocacy, these groups can help reshape higher education for the better, ensuring that it continues to provide opportunities for social mobility and success for future generations.

Students as Advocates for Change

Students must be at the forefront of the movement for higher education reform, as they are the primary beneficiaries of the system. Their experiences within the education system, from rising tuition costs to the challenges posed by student debt, give them a unique perspective and a strong interest in ensuring that the system works for them. As the future of the workforce and society, students have a vested interest in ensuring that their education is both affordable and relevant. Through collective action, students can have a powerful impact on reshaping higher education, demanding change from administrators, policymakers, and faculty to address the inequities and inefficiencies that currently plague the system.

Using Collective Voice for Policy Change

Student organizations, particularly those focused on advocating for first-generation, low-income, and underrepresented students, are well-positioned to push for meaningful policy changes. By organizing protests, petitions, and advocacy campaigns, students can raise awareness about the growing financial burdens they face and advocate for policies that address rising tuition costs, the increasing levels of student debt, and the need for greater institutional accountability. Through grassroots movements, students can demand action from both their institutions and government entities, calling for tuition freezes or reductions, student loan reform, and increased funding for public higher education.

Students' voices can be especially powerful when they come together to speak on behalf of their peers, representing diverse communities and addressing the common challenges they face. Student-led organizations can push for changes that benefit all students, including calls for more accessible mental health services, affordable textbooks, and improved support systems for students from marginalized backgrounds. Moreover, students can advocate for transparent pricing and clearer communication around financial aid options, ensuring that future students are not blindsided by rising costs or unclear financial obligations.

Student-Faculty Partnerships for Institutional Reform

In addition to organizing for policy reform, students can play an instrumental role in shaping institutional changes through dialogue and collaboration with faculty and administrators. Engaging in constructive conversations with these groups allows students to advocate for curriculum reforms, increased academic support, and better campus policies that directly affect their daily lives and academic success. Establishing formal and informal partnerships between students and faculty can help ensure that reforms are not only about reducing costs but also improving the quality of education and the overall student experience.

For example, students can work with faculty to advocate for the inclusion of experiential learning opportunities in the curriculum, such as internships, co-ops, or field-based learning, which give students the practical skills and experience they need to succeed in their careers. By having a say in curriculum development, students ensure that their education is not just theoretical but aligned with the demands of the modern workforce. Furthermore, students can also push for reforms that address the personal well-being of students, such as better mental health services, support for nontraditional students, and policies that foster inclusivity and diversity on campus.

In essence, students have the potential to be powerful agents of change within their institutions. By organizing, lobbying, and collaborating with faculty, they can ensure that higher education is affordable, inclusive, and responsive to the needs of the students it serves.

Faculty as Leaders in Educational Reform

Faculty members are the cornerstone of any educational system, providing the knowledge, expertise, and mentorship that students need to succeed. As the primary educators and influencers within the academic environment, faculty are uniquely positioned to lead and drive the reform efforts that will reshape higher education. They must take an active role in advocating for changes that address both the content and delivery of education, ensuring that students are equipped not only with theoretical knowledge but also with the practical skills and experiences they need to thrive in the modern workforce.

Innovative Teaching Models

Faculty must embrace innovative teaching models that better meet the needs of a diverse student body. Traditional teaching methods, which often rely on one-size-fits-all approaches and large lecture-based courses, may not effectively engage students or address the various learning styles and needs that exist in the classroom. Faculty should advocate for smaller class sizes, which allow for more individualized instruction and the development of stronger relationships between students and professors. This personalization can lead to improved academic outcomes and greater student satisfaction.

In addition, faculty should be open to adopting new teaching methods that focus on active learning, collaborative projects, and problem-solving. This could involve incorporating flipped classrooms, where students review content outside of class and engage in discussion or projects during class time, or using case studies and real-world scenarios to make learning more relevant and applicable. The goal should be to create an environment where students are not passive recipients of information but active participants in their learning process.

Preparing Students for a Global Economy

Another crucial role for faculty in higher education reform is to ensure that students are prepared for a global economy. This can be achieved by fostering a broader, more inclusive curriculum that emphasizes the development of critical thinking, cross-cultural competencies, and the ability to work in diverse, multicultural teams. Faculty can incorporate global perspectives into their courses, teaching students about international issues, global trends, and the interconnectedness of the world's economies. This will help students understand that they must be equipped not only with technical skills but also with the ability to navigate a rapidly changing and diverse global landscape.

Furthermore, faculty should advocate for incorporating experiential learning opportunities into academic programs. This might include internships, service learning projects, global exchange programs, or collaborative partnerships with industry that give students hands-on experience and practical exposure to their chosen fields. These opportunities provide students with valuable insights into the workforce while developing skills that go beyond the classroom. By working with industry leaders and policymakers, faculty can ensure that academic programs align with the skills and knowledge that employers are seeking, making students more competitive in the job market (Ehrenberg, 2012).

Faculty's Role in Shaping Institutional Policies

Faculty members also have an important role in advocating for institutional policies that support academic excellence and student success. By participating in governance structures, faculty can help shape decisions related to curriculum development, faculty hiring, and student services. Faculty should work with administrators to ensure that policies are student-centered and reflect the evolving needs of both the student body and the workforce.

Faculty members can also push for policies that support equity and inclusion on campus. By promoting diversity in their own teaching practices, advocating for equitable admissions policies, and supporting initiatives that serve underrepresented groups, faculty help create a more inclusive and supportive learning environment. Their leadership in these areas is essential to ensure that all students, regardless of background, have the resources and opportunities needed to succeed.

Leading Change for a More Inclusive Future

In summary, faculty must be leaders in the movement for higher education reform. By embracing innovative teaching methods, advocating for curriculum reform, and engaging in institutional governance, faculty members can ensure that higher education evolves to meet the needs of today's students and the demands of the global economy. Faculty's influence on the academic culture and student experience is profound, and their active participation in reform efforts will help create a more inclusive, affordable, and relevant higher education system.

Reinventing Higher Education as a Tool for Equity, Opportunity, and Societal Progress

In the face of mounting challenges, higher education must undergo a fundamental reinvention to fulfill its original mission of promoting opportunity and societal progress. Historically, higher education has been viewed as a powerful engine of upward mobility, offering individuals the chance to improve their lives and contribute to the greater good of society. However, the rising costs of tuition, the ballooning student debt crisis, and the increasing disconnect between educational outcomes and workforce needs have undermined this promise. These issues have made higher education less accessible and less effective in preparing students for the realities of the modern economy. To reclaim higher education's potential as a tool for social equity and individual advancement, it is critical to refocus on its core mission: to empower individuals, foster community development, and contribute to the common good.

Promoting Equity Through Access and Affordability

One of the most pressing challenges in reinventing higher education is ensuring that it remains accessible to all, regardless of socioeconomic background. For higher education to serve its fundamental purpose of providing opportunities for upward mobility, it must be affordable. The escalating cost of tuition has been a major barrier to access for many students, especially those from low-income families. The current financial aid system, while helpful, often fails to adequately support students in need, and the increasing burden of student loans only exacerbates the issue. It is therefore essential that we prioritize policies and reforms that reduce the cost of education while expanding access to financial aid.

Governments and institutions must take the lead in addressing these disparities. One solution is the implementation of free community college programs, which would provide students from all backgrounds the opportunity to pursue higher education without incurring debt. Programs like Tennessee Promise have shown that free community college can significantly increase enrollment, particularly among students from lower-income families (Dynarski et al., 2018). In addition to free tuition programs, expanding income-driven repayment plans for federal student loans can help alleviate the burden of debt for graduates by tying loan payments to their income, ensuring that students are not saddled with unmanageable debt.

At the same time, financial aid policies must be restructured to better support the most vulnerable populations, including students of color, first-generation college students, and those from rural or marginalized communities. These students often face multiple barriers to success, including financial insecurity, lack of familial support, and fewer academic resources. Increasing the availability of scholarships, grants, and targeted financial aid programs would ensure that all students, regardless of their background, have the resources they need to succeed in higher education.

However, access to higher education must not be viewed in isolation. It is just as important that institutions create environments that foster diversity, inclusion, and equity. Access is only meaningful if students feel welcome, supported, and able to succeed. Universities and colleges must cultivate inclusive campuses that actively engage with students from diverse backgrounds, ensuring that everyone has the opportunity to thrive. This includes providing services such as mentoring, counseling, and academic support, which can help students overcome obstacles and stay on track academically. In particular, services tailored to the needs of first-generation students, students of color, and those from low-income backgrounds are critical to creating an environment in which all students can succeed.

Promoting Opportunity Through Workforce Alignment

In addition to promoting access and affordability, higher education must also ensure that students are prepared for the workforce. To fulfill its promise of helping students achieve long-term financial stability, higher education must align more closely with the needs of the modern economy. For too long, colleges and universities have operated in a silo, with academic curricula often out of sync with the realities of the labor market. Employers across industries—from technology to healthcare—are increasingly seeking graduates with practical skills, and educational institutions must rise to the challenge of meeting these demands.

One key step in aligning education with workforce needs is the development of strong partnerships between educational institutions and industries. By working closely with businesses, universities can create curricula that respond to emerging job markets and equip students with the skills that are in high demand. For example, universities can collaborate with tech companies to design courses in artificial intelligence, cybersecurity, and data analytics, or partner with healthcare providers to develop programs focused on nursing, medical research, and public health. At the same time, it is essential that liberal arts and social sciences programs continue to be valued, as these disciplines foster critical thinking, creativity, and leadership—skills that are vital for the innovation and problem-solving required in any field.

Higher education must also promote lifelong learning by offering flexible educational pathways for individuals throughout their careers. As industries evolve, so too must the skills of the workforce. Universities can help meet this need by offering certifications, micro-credentials, and online learning opportunities that allow workers to continuously update their skills and remain competitive in their careers. These alternative pathways are particularly important for nontraditional students—those who are returning to education after time in the workforce, or who are looking to shift careers. Providing affordable, accessible ways for individuals to gain new skills ensures that higher education serves not only traditional students but also workers seeking to upskill or re-skill in an ever-changing job market.

By creating educational pathways that better align with career opportunities, higher education can play a critical role in promoting economic mobility and providing individuals with the tools they need to succeed. Students who graduate with practical, marketable skills will be better positioned to secure stable, high-paying jobs, leading to long-term financial security and contributing to a stronger, more resilient economy. Moreover, when universities focus on workforce alignment, they can help address pressing social needs, such as filling the demand for healthcare professionals, engineers, and teachers, and preparing students to contribute meaningfully to society.

Building a Holistic Vision of Higher Education

Reinventing higher education requires a vision that goes beyond just improving access or workforce alignment. It demands a shift in focus toward a more holistic understanding of what higher education is for: empowering individuals, strengthening communities, and fostering societal progress. By promoting equity, opportunity, and workforce alignment, higher education can fulfill its historical mission of creating a more just and prosperous society.

This reinvention is not solely the responsibility of governments or institutions but requires a collective effort from all sectors—public, private, and academic. Together, these groups must work to reshape higher education into an inclusive, accessible, and dynamic force for good. By fostering an educational system that not only prepares students for careers but also nurtures the qualities that contribute to a thriving, equitable society, we can ensure that higher education remains a powerful tool for individual advancement and societal progress for generations to come.

Fostering Societal Progress Through Social Responsibility

In the 21st century, higher education must transcend its traditional role of simply preparing students for careers. It must evolve into a powerful force for societal progress, actively contributing to the solutions of the world's most pressing challenges. Whether it is tackling climate change, addressing systemic social inequalities, improving public health outcomes, or advancing human rights, universities are uniquely positioned to lead the way in creating a more just, equitable, and sustainable world. This vision of higher education as a vehicle for social responsibility calls for an intentional and comprehensive approach—one that integrates societal issues into academic curricula, fosters civic engagement, and empowers students to become proactive citizens who contribute positively to the global community.

Embedding Global Issues into the Curriculum

One of the most effective ways for higher education to foster societal progress is by embedding issues of global importance into the core curriculum. By incorporating topics such as climate change, social justice, public health, and global human rights into academic programs, universities can ensure that students are not only learning specific skills but also gaining a broader understanding of the challenges that the world faces. These issues are not isolated; they are interconnected, and students need to grasp how these global challenges affect every aspect of society, from economics and politics to individual well-being and environmental sustainability.

For example, universities can create interdisciplinary programs that combine fields like environmental science, economics, and policy studies to address the complexities of climate change. In addition, integrating courses that focus on race, equity, and justice can help students understand the root causes of social inequalities and inspire them to think critically about how to dismantle systems of oppression. Public health courses can emphasize the importance of global health initiatives and the ways in which healthcare access and quality vary across different populations and regions. By weaving these issues into the fabric of academic curricula, universities can prepare students to tackle real-world problems with the knowledge and skills they need to effect change.

Moreover, these issues should not be confined to specialized programs but should be a part of the general education requirements for all students. Regardless of their major, every student should have exposure to topics that teach them about the pressing issues of our time and the ways in which they can contribute to solving them. This type of education ensures that graduates are not only technically proficient in their fields but also socially aware and globally minded.

Encouraging Civic Engagement and Activism

Higher education must also create opportunities for students to engage directly with the issues they study through community service, activism, and social justice initiatives. While academic knowledge is essential, practical engagement is equally important in developing the leadership skills and social responsibility necessary to drive societal change. Universities should offer programs that encourage students to volunteer, participate in internships, and work with nonprofit organizations or government agencies focused on addressing key societal challenges.

For instance, service-learning programs, which integrate community service with academic coursework, provide students with the opportunity to apply their learning in real-world contexts. Students can work on projects related to social justice, environmental conservation, public health, or education, directly benefiting local communities while gaining invaluable experience. These programs not only contribute to the students' personal growth but also help build stronger, more connected communities by addressing unmet needs.

Additionally, universities should encourage student activism, where students can organize around causes they care about and advocate for policy changes that align with their values. From climate strikes to campaigns for racial justice, student activism has historically played a critical role in social progress, and universities can provide a platform for students to mobilize and make their voices heard. In doing so, higher education institutions can inspire students to take ownership of the issues they care about and empower them to become agents of change both within their communities and on a global scale.

Developing Global Citizens

In an increasingly interconnected world, universities must also prepare students to be global citizens who understand and respect the cultures, perspectives, and challenges of others. This includes offering opportunities for international study, research, and service learning. Studying abroad, for example, gives students the chance to immerse themselves in different cultures, deepen their understanding of global issues, and engage with people from diverse backgrounds. These experiences foster empathy and a broader worldview, which are essential for addressing complex global challenges.

Moreover, universities should emphasize the importance of global cooperation and the need for interdisciplinary approaches to solving problems. Many of the most urgent issues facing the world today, such as climate change, public health pandemics, and economic inequality, require coordinated efforts across borders. By teaching students to think globally, universities can cultivate a generation of leaders who are equipped to work collaboratively with others—across cultures, sectors, and disciplines—to find solutions that benefit humanity as a whole.

Integrating Ethics and Social Responsibility into Professional Development

Finally, higher education must prioritize the integration of ethics and social responsibility into professional development. As students progress in their academic and professional careers, they must be encouraged to consider the broader ethical implications of their work. Whether they are pursuing careers in business, healthcare, engineering, or the arts, students should be equipped with the tools to make ethical decisions and contribute to societal well-being in their respective fields.

For instance, business schools can teach students about corporate social responsibility (CSR) and the importance of ethical business practices that prioritize long-term societal benefits over short-term profits. Medical and public health programs can emphasize the importance of equity in healthcare access and the ethical considerations of clinical practice. Similarly, engineering programs can teach students to think about the social impact of technological innovations and to design solutions that benefit society while minimizing harm to the environment or vulnerable populations.

By instilling a strong sense of social responsibility in students as they move from the classroom to their careers, higher education can ensure that graduates understand the power they hold to influence society and are committed to using their knowledge and skills to contribute to the common good.

Higher Education as a Force for Good

Reimagining higher education as a tool for societal progress requires a broad and integrated approach that addresses not only the individual needs of students but also the collective needs of society. By embedding global issues into the curriculum, encouraging civic engagement and activism, fostering global citizenship, and promoting ethical professional development, universities can create a generation of students who are not only prepared for successful careers but also equipped to address the world's most pressing challenges. This reinvention of higher education is essential for building a more just, equitable, and sustainable world, ensuring that education continues to serve as a powerful force for social progress and the common good.

As we look to the future of higher education, the need for bold, transformative action has never been clearer. By fostering collaboration between governments, the private sector, and academic institutions, we can begin to dismantle the barriers that limit access, inflate costs, and perpetuate inequality. The responsibility lies not only with policymakers and institutions but also with alumni, students, and faculty, whose voices and actions can drive the reforms necessary to create a more inclusive and equitable system. By reinventing higher education as a tool for social progress, opportunity, and empowerment, we can ensure that it remains a beacon of hope and a catalyst for positive change in society. The time for reform is now, and together, we can chart a course toward a more just, accessible, and sustainable future for all.

Chapter 16

Reviving the American Dream

As America faces unprecedented challenges—economic inequality, social injustice, and a rapidly evolving global economy—the role of higher education in shaping the future of the nation has never been more critical. For generations, higher education has been seen as the cornerstone of the American Dream, offering individuals the opportunity to rise above their circumstances and build better lives for themselves and their families. Yet, in recent decades, the promise of higher education has been undermined by rising costs, student debt, and a disconnect between the skills students acquire and the needs of the workforce. As a result, the dream of upward mobility through education is increasingly out of reach for many.

This chapter explores the urgent need to revive higher education as a force for good—a tool for equity, opportunity, and societal progress. It outlines the systemic flaws that have hindered higher education's ability to fulfill its core mission and provides a hopeful vision for a future where colleges and universities once again serve as pillars of opportunity, innovation, and social change. The revival of higher education is not only necessary to restore the promise of the American Dream but is also vital for the future of America itself.

Higher Education's Role in Shaping the Future of America

For generations, higher education has been seen as the cornerstone of the American Dream—a vehicle for individual advancement, a bridge to opportunity, and a path to financial security. The promise of higher education has motivated countless students to aspire for something greater than what they were born into, to achieve their dreams, and to build a life of stability and success. It has been central to the notion that anyone, regardless of their background, can achieve success through hard work, education, and perseverance. Higher education, in its ideal form, was always meant to be a leveler of inequalities, a means of propelling individuals from disadvantaged backgrounds into positions of influence, power, and wealth. The American Dream was, for many, synonymous with higher education.

However, this vision of higher education has been increasingly undermined by rising costs, student debt, and a growing disconnect between the skills students acquire and the needs of the modern workforce. Over the past few decades, as college tuition has risen sharply and student loan debt has ballooned, the promise of higher education has often felt more like a burden than a boon. Students from lower-income backgrounds are now more likely to face crippling debt than ever before, and even those who graduate are finding it more difficult to find jobs that allow them to thrive.

Still, higher education's potential to shape the future of America is not lost. In fact, it remains as critical as ever to the future of the nation. The role of higher education extends beyond merely providing individuals with skills for employment; it is about shaping the broader societal landscape. Universities are not only places of learning; they are incubators for innovation, research, and progress. They are hubs for social and cultural development, producing leaders in fields like technology, healthcare, the arts, and business who will confront the challenges of tomorrow. Higher education also plays an essential role in fostering democratic values, critical thinking, and civic engagement. Students leave colleges and universities not only with degrees but with the tools to challenge the status quo, to ask tough questions, and to shape the future for the better.

As America faces unprecedented challenges in the 21st century, including climate change, economic inequality, and a rapidly changing job market, the role of higher education is more significant than ever. Institutions of higher learning must adapt to serve the needs of the nation by producing graduates who are not only prepared for the workforce but also equipped with the intellectual and ethical tools to address the complex issues facing the world today.

Urgency of Addressing Systemic Flaws to Prevent Further Decline

While higher education has the potential to shape the future, its current trajectory threatens to exacerbate the divisions already present in American society. The systemic flaws within the system are profound and urgent, and they require immediate attention to prevent further decline. If left unchecked, these flaws could undermine the ability of higher education to fulfill its role as a foundation of opportunity and a force for social mobility.

The rising cost of college education is perhaps the most glaring of these systemic issues. With tuition rates skyrocketing and student loan debt reaching over $1.7 trillion, the financial burden of attending college has become untenable for many families. The very institutions meant to uplift individuals and promote equality are, in fact, creating greater divides between socioeconomic classes. Students from lower-income families are increasingly locked out of the opportunities provided by higher education because of the prohibitive costs. At the same time, middle-class families are often forced to take on significant debt just to afford a degree, while wealthier students have access to greater resources and opportunities that make the journey through higher education easier and more affordable.

Moreover, the rise of student debt has led to a generation of young adults who, instead of building wealth and investing in their future, are instead burdened by the weight of loans that often take decades to repay. This financial strain not only impacts individuals but also has broader economic consequences. When graduates are saddled with debt, their purchasing power is reduced, affecting everything from housing markets to consumer spending. The debt burden also has a long-lasting impact on personal well-being, with students reporting higher levels of stress and mental health challenges due to their financial obligations.

Beyond the financial crisis, higher education faces the challenge of a growing disconnect between the skills that students acquire and the needs of the workforce. While some universities have begun to address this issue by integrating career-oriented programs and partnerships with industries, too many institutions still focus on traditional, theoretical education that leaves students ill-prepared for the rapidly evolving job market. In today's economy, where industries like technology, healthcare, and green energy are experiencing rapid growth, universities must ensure that their curricula are aligned with these emerging fields, providing students with the practical skills necessary to succeed in these high-demand sectors.

Furthermore, the increasing reliance on adjunct faculty, rather than tenured professors, has compromised the quality of education in many institutions. Adjuncts, often paid low wages and given minimal job security, are typically overworked and under-resourced, limiting their ability to offer students the attention and support they need. This shift away from full-time, tenure-track faculty has weakened the academic rigor and overall educational experience, further diminishing the value of a degree.

The urgency of addressing these systemic flaws cannot be overstated. If higher education is to remain a pillar of opportunity and innovation, significant reforms are required in areas such as tuition pricing, student debt management, workforce alignment, and the treatment of faculty. Without these reforms, higher education will continue to perpetuate inequalities, leaving millions of students unable to access the opportunities they deserve.

Hopeful Vision for the Revival of Colleges and Universities as Pillars of Opportunity and Innovation

Despite the many challenges, there is hope for the future of higher education in America. If higher education is to be reinvigorated and restored to its core mission of opportunity and societal progress, it will require bold and transformative changes. But these changes are not only necessary—they are achievable. There is a vision for the revival of colleges and universities as dynamic, inclusive, and innovative institutions that prepare students for success in the 21st century while addressing the urgent needs of society.

Affordable and Accessible Education

The first step toward reviving the American Dream through higher education is making it more affordable and accessible. This involves both reducing the cost of education and expanding access to financial aid for all students. One promising approach is to expand free community college programs, which have already proven successful in states like Tennessee and Oregon. By providing tuition-free community college education, we can ensure that students from all backgrounds, particularly those from low-income families, have access to higher education without accumulating debilitating debt.

Additionally, reforms to the federal student loan system, such as income-driven repayment plans and loan forgiveness programs, would allow graduates to pay back loans in a way that reflects their earning potential. These programs would help ensure that students are not burdened by excessive debt and can focus on building their careers and contributing to society.

Curriculum and Workforce Alignment

Another key component of higher education reform is ensuring that academic curricula are aligned with the needs of the modern workforce. Universities must work closely with industries to design programs that equip students with the skills that are in high demand. This means expanding programs in fields such as healthcare, technology, and green energy, while also ensuring that liberal arts programs continue to develop critical thinking, creativity, and leadership. A strong partnership between academia and industry can lead to job-ready graduates who contribute to economic growth and societal progress.

Incorporating experiential learning, internships, and apprenticeships into curricula is also essential. These hands-on experiences not only provide students with practical skills but also increase their employability and help bridge the gap between academic learning and real-world application. By offering students a blend of theoretical knowledge and practical experience, universities can create graduates who are not only well-educated but also well-prepared to meet the demands of the job market.

Social Responsibility and Civic Engagement

Finally, higher education must prioritize the development of socially responsible and engaged citizens. Universities should embed social responsibility into their curricula, encouraging students to engage with issues such as climate change, social justice, and public health. By fostering a culture of civic engagement and activism, universities can inspire students to become leaders who are committed to solving the world's most pressing challenges.

By integrating these principles into the core mission of higher education, universities can become not just places of learning but engines of social change. They can produce graduates who are not only skilled professionals but also ethical leaders who are dedicated to creating a more just, equitable, and sustainable world.

Restoring Opportunity in Higher Education

The future of higher education in America hinges on our ability to reform the system and realign it with the core values of opportunity, equity, and societal progress. The current system is undeniably broken—too many students face rising costs, crushing debt, and an education that fails to prepare them for the demands of the modern workforce. However, through bold, innovative reforms, we can revive the American Dream by restoring higher education as a powerful tool for social mobility, community development, and economic growth.

One critical area for reform is ensuring that community colleges, universities, and technical institutions stop creating degrees of little to no value in the workforce. Community colleges must move away from turning technical trades into Associate of Science (AS) and Associate of Applied Science (AAS) degrees solely to generate revenue. These practices mislead students, burden them with unnecessary debt, and dilute the value of technical training. Instead, colleges should focus on offering pathways that are directly aligned with employer needs and market demands. Universities must also scrutinize their degree offerings to ensure they provide tangible value to students and society, eliminating programs that fail to prepare graduates for meaningful employment.

Moreover, the pervasive reliance on general education course requirements to prop up outdated academic fields must be reconsidered. This approach often serves as a financial lifeline for departments that no longer align with workforce demands, rather than serving the best interests of students. Higher education institutions should streamline curricula to prioritize skills and knowledge that equip students for real-world challenges, ensuring every course contributes meaningfully to their career readiness and personal growth.

The cost of higher education must also be confronted directly. If pursuing a bachelor's degree leads to $250,000 in student loans, a master's degree adds another $100,000, and a bachelor's through PhD results in nearly $500,000 in debt, then something has gone terribly wrong. These staggering figures reflect a system out of balance, where the promise of education is overshadowed by unsustainable financial burdens. Reform must address not only the affordability of tuition but also the long-term value and financial viability of the degrees offered.

By making education more affordable, aligning curricula with workforce needs, and fostering a culture of social responsibility, we can ensure that higher education continues to serve as the gateway to opportunity for all students. Reforming the system isn't just about cost—it's about value. Institutions must take responsibility for providing programs that are relevant, effective, and equitable, empowering students with the skills and knowledge they need to succeed in an ever-evolving job market.

Finally, the path forward for higher education in America is clear: bold, transformative reform is not just necessary, but imperative for the revival of the American Dream. Education has long been a beacon of opportunity, yet its promise has been overshadowed by systemic inefficiencies, misaligned priorities, and crippling debt. The time has come to restore higher education's central role in society, ensuring that it once again serves as a vehicle for upward mobility, economic opportunity, and societal progress. By addressing these challenges with decisive action, we can create a future where higher education empowers individuals, strengthens communities, and serves as the cornerstone of opportunity and innovation for generations to come.

Bibliography

Abel, J. R., & Deitz, R. (2022). Despite rising costs, college is still a good investment—but not always. Federal Reserve Bank of New York. https://www.newyorkfed.org

Addo, F. R., Houle, J. N., & Simon, D. (2016). Young, Black, and (still) in the red: Parental wealth, race, and student loan debt. Race and Social Problems, 8(1), 64-76. https://doi.org/10.1007/s12552-016-9162-0

Advance CTE. (2020). State CTE funding policies and practices. Retrieved from https://www.careertech.org

Altbach, P. G. (2011). The global academic revolution: The rise of the research university and its academic impact. Johns Hopkins University Press.

Ambrose, B. W., Cordell, L., & Ma, S. (2021). The impact of student debt on homeownership. Journal of Urban Economics, 122, 103-112. https://doi.org/10.1016/j.jue.2021.103112

American College Health Association (ACHA). (2021). National College Health Assessment III: Undergraduate student reference group executive summary spring 2021. Retrieved from https://www.acha.org

American Federation of Teachers. (2020). An army of temps: AFT 2020 adjunct faculty survey.

American Psychological Association. (2022). Stress in America: Financial stress and student loans. https://www.apa.org

Bailey, T. R., Jaggars, S. S., & Jenkins, D. (2015). Redesigning America's community colleges: A clearer path to student success. Harvard University Press.

Baum, S. (2016). Student debt: Rhetoric and realities of higher education financing. Palgrave Macmillan.

Baum, S., & Ma, J. (2020). Trends in college pricing and student aid. The College Board.

Bertrand, M., & Mullainathan, S. (2004). Are Emily and Greg more employable than Lakisha and Jamal? A field experiment on labor market discrimination. American Economic Review, 94(4), 991–1013. https://doi.org/10.1257/0002828042002561

Bettinger, E. P., & Long, B. T. (2010). Does cheaper mean better? The impact of using adjunct instructors on student outcomes. Review of Economics and Statistics, 92(3), 598–613.

Bok, D. (2003). Universities in the marketplace: The commercialization of higher education. Princeton University Press.

Bound, J., & Turner, S. (2002). Going to war and going to college: Did World War II and the GI Bill increase educational attainment for returning veterans? Journal of Labor Economics, 20(4), 784-815. https://doi.org/10.1086/342012

Burning Glass Technologies. (2017). The disappearing degree: How the job market is changing. Retrieved from https://www.burning-glass.com

Bureau of Labor Statistics. (2022). Occupational employment and wage statistics. U.S. Department of Labor. Retrieved from https://www.bls.gov

Bureau of Labor Statistics. (2023). Occupational outlook handbook: Social workers. U.S. Department of Labor. https://www.bls.gov/ooh/community-and-social-service/social-workers.htm

Bureau of Labor Statistics. (2023). Occupational outlook handbook: Reporters, correspondents, and broadcast news analysts. U.S. Department of Labor. https://www.bls.gov/ooh/media-and-communication/reporters-correspondents-and-broadcast-news-analysts.htm

California State Auditor. (2017). The University of California: Its admissions and financial decisions have disadvantaged California resident students.

Carnevale, A. P., Smith, N., & Strohl, J. (2010). Help wanted: Projections of jobs and education requirements through 2018. Georgetown University Center on Education and the Workforce.

Carnevale, A. P., Rose, S. J., & Cheah, B. (2021). The college payoff: Education, occupations, lifetime earnings. Georgetown University Center on Education and the Workforce. Retrieved from https://cew.georgetown.edu

Carnevale, A. P., Rose, S. J., & Hanson, A. R. (2021). The unfulfilled promise of community colleges. Georgetown University Center on Education and the Workforce.

Carnevale, A. P., Smith, N., & Strohl, J. (2012). Recovery: Job growth and education requirements through 2020. Georgetown University Center on Education and the Workforce.

Cassuto, L. (2021). The graduate school mess: What caused it and how we can fix it. Harvard University Press.

Cellini, S. R., & Turner, N. (2019). Gainfully employed? Assessing the employment and earnings of for-profit college students using administrative data. Journal of Human Resources, 54(2), 342–370.

Cellini, S. R., & Turner, N. (2016). Gainfully employed? Assessing the employment and earnings of for-profit college students using administrative data. Journal of Human Resources, 51(2), 342–370. https://doi.org/10.3368/jhr.51.2.342

Chetty, R., Friedman, J. N., Saez, E., Turner, N., & Yagan, D. (2017). Mobility report cards: The role of colleges in intergenerational mobility. Quarterly Journal of Economics, 133(3), 1107–1163. https://doi.org/10.1093/qje/qjy009

Clark, C. (2018). The role of safe spaces in higher education: Balancing inclusion and intellectual freedom. Journal of Diversity in Higher Education, 11(2), 107–120. https://doi.org/10.1037/dhe0000069

Clemson Faculty Senate Report. (2022). Concerns over budget allocation and academic prioritization. Clemson University Senate Archives.

Cohen, A. M., Brawer, F. B., & Kisker, C. B. (2014). The American community college (6th ed.). Jossey-Bass.

College Board. (2021). Trends in college pricing and student aid 2021. Retrieved from https://research.collegeboard.org

Collins, R. (2019). Credential inflation and the future of work: Understanding the risks of overqualification. Sociology of Education, 92(2), 165–180. https://doi.org/10.1177/0038040719853841

Collinge, A. (2009). The student loan scam: The most oppressive debt in U.S. history—and how we can fight back. Beacon Press.

Complete College America. (2023). About us. Retrieved from https://completecollege.org

Consumer Financial Protection Bureau. (2021). What is a reasonable debt-to-income ratio for student loans? https://www.consumerfinance.gov

Consumer Financial Protection Bureau. (2022). Navient settlement: What student loan borrowers need to know. Retrieved from https://www.consumerfinance.gov

Corrigan, P. W., Druss, B. G., & Perlick, D. A. (2014). The impact of mental illness stigma on seeking and participating in mental health care. Psychological Science in the Public Interest, 15(2), 37–70. https://doi.org/10.1177/1529100614531398

Delbanco, A. (2012). College: What it was, is, and should be. Princeton University Press.

Desrochers, D. M., & Kirshstein, R. J. (2014). Labor intensive or labor expensive? Changing staffing and compensation patterns in higher education. Delta Cost Project.

Dougherty, K. J., & Reddy, V. (2013). Performance funding for higher education: What are the mechanisms? What are the impacts? ASHE Higher Education Report, 39(2), 1–134.

Duderstadt, J. J. (2000). A university for the 21st century. University of Michigan Press.

Dynarski, S., Scott-Clayton, J., & Wiederspan, M. (2018). Simplifying tax incentives and aid for college: Progress and prospects. National Tax Journal, 71(2), 299–318.

Ehrenberg, R. G. (2012). Tuition rising: Why college costs so much. Harvard University Press.

Eide, S. (2018). Administrative bloat at America's colleges and universities: The real reason tuition is skyrocketing. Manhattan Institute.

Eisenberg, D., Lipson, S. K., & Heinze, J. (2019). The Healthy Minds Study: Understanding the mental health of college students. Journal of Adolescent Health, 64(5), 564–570. https://doi.org/10.1016/j.jadohealth.2019.02.013

Engle, J., & Tinto, V. (2008). Moving beyond access: College success for low-income, first-generation students. Pell Institute for the Study of Opportunity in Higher Education.

Etzkowitz, H. (2008). The triple helix: University-industry-government innovation in action. Routledge.

Federal Reserve. (2020). Economic well-being of U.S. households in 2019. Board of Governors of the Federal Reserve System.

Federal Reserve. (2021). Economic well-being of U.S. households in 2020. https://www.federalreserve.gov/publications/2021-economic-well-being-of-us-households.htm

Federal Reserve Bank of New York. (2023). Quarterly report on household debt and credit.

Federal Student Aid. (2023). Understanding repayment. U.S. Department of Education. https://studentaid.gov/manage-loans/repayment

Friedman, Z. (2023). U.S. student loan debt statistics 2024. Forbes. Retrieved from https://www.forbes.com

Geiger, R. L. (2017). Research and relevant knowledge: American research universities since World War II. Transaction Publishers.

Ginsberg, B. (2011). The fall of the faculty: The rise of the all-administrative university and why it matters. Oxford University Press.

Goldrick-Rab, S. (2016). Paying the price: College costs, financial aid, and the betrayal of the American dream. University of Chicago Press.

Goldrick-Rab, S., Baker-Smith, C., Coca, V., Looker, E., & Williams, T. (2020). College and university basic needs insecurity: A national #RealCollege survey report. The Hope Center for College, Community, and Justice. Retrieved from https://hope4college.com

Hersh, R. H., & Keeling, R. P. (2013). We're losing our minds: Rethinking American higher education. Palgrave Macmillan.

Higher Education Research Institute (HERI). (2018). Faculty survey: Political ideologies of professors. Retrieved from https://heri.ucla.edu

Higher Education Financial Trends Report. (2023). Administrative growth and spending patterns in public universities.

Hillman, N., Tandberg, D., & Gross, J. P. (2015). Performance funding in higher education: Do financial incentives impact college completions? Journal of Higher Education, 85(6), 826–857.

Hiss, W., & Franks, V. (2014). Defining promise: Optional standardized testing policies in American college and university admissions. National Association for College Admission Counseling.

Huelsman, M. (2018). The unaffordable era: How the student debt crisis is reshaping America. Demos.

Huelsman, M. (2018). The unbearable cost of student loan debt. Demos.

Hurwitz, M. (2011). The impact of legacy status on undergraduate admissions at elite colleges and universities. Economics of Education Review, 30(3), 480–492. https://doi.org/10.1016/j.econedurev.2010.12.002

Hutcheson, P. A. (2007). A people's history of American higher education. Vanderbilt University Press.

Inbar, Y., & Lammers, J. (2012). Political diversity in social and personality psychology. Perspectives on Psychological Science, 7(5), 496–503. https://doi.org/10.1177/1745691612455206

Jacob, B. A., McCall, B., & Stange, K. (2013). College as country club: Do colleges cater to students' preferences for consumption? National Bureau of Economic Research.

Jenkins, D., & Fink, J. (2015). What we know about transfer. Community College Research Center.

Jenkins, D., & Fink, J. (2016). Tracking transfer: Measures of effectiveness in helping community college students to complete bachelor's degrees. Community College Research Center.

Kelchen, R. (2018). Higher education accountability. Johns Hopkins University Press.

Kelchen, R. (2021). Higher education accountability. Johns Hopkins University Press.

Kezar, A., DePaola, T., & Scott, D. T. (2019). The gig academy: Mapping labor in the neoliberal university. Johns Hopkins University Press.

Kimball, B. A. (1995). Orators and philosophers: A history of the idea of liberal education. The Liberal Arts Tradition: A Documentary History. University Press of America.

Knight Foundation. (2019). Free expression on college campuses: What do students think? Retrieved from https://knightfoundation.org

Kuh, G. D., Kinzie, J., Buckley, J. A., Bridges, B. K., & Hayek, J. C. (2011). Student success in college: Creating conditions that matter. Jossey-Bass.

Labaree, D. F. (2017). A perfect mess: The unintended consequences of educational reform. University of Chicago Press.

Levin, J. S., Kater, S., & Wagoner, R. L. (2010). Community college faculty: At work in the new economy. Palgrave Macmillan.

Looney, A., & Yannelis, C. (2019). The consequences of student loan debt: Evidence from default and repayment behavior. Brookings Papers on Economic Activity, 2019(1), 1-89.

Looney, A., & Yannelis, C. (2020). The consequences of student loan credit expansions: Evidence from three decades of default cycles. American Economic Journal: Economic Policy, 12(1), 297–328.

Looney, A., & Yannelis, C. (2022). The consequences of student loan debt. Brookings Institution. https://www.brookings.edu

Manyika, J., Chui, M., Miremadi, M., Bughin, J., George, K., Willmott, P., & Dewhurst, M. (2017). Harnessing automation for a future that works. McKinsey & Company. https://www.mckinsey.com

Mettler, S. (2005). Soldiers to citizens: The GI Bill and the making of the greatest generation. Oxford University Press.

Mezza, A., Ringo, D., Sherlund, S. M., & Sommer, K. (2020). Student loans and homeownership. Journal of Labor Economics, 38(1), 215-260. https://doi.org/10.1086/704606

Miller, B., Campbell, C., & Cohen, B. (2019). The road to zero: A vision for debt-free college. Center for American Progress.

Miller, B., & Erwin, B. (2020). Community colleges and bachelor's degrees: Supporting students and addressing workforce needs. Education Commission of the States. Retrieved from https://www.ecs.org

Mitchell, J. (2021). The debt trap: How student loans became a national catastrophe. Simon & Schuster.

Mitchell, M., Leachman, M., & Masterson, K. (2019). A lost decade in higher education funding. Center on Budget and Policy Priorities.

Mitchell, M., Leachman, M., & Masterson, K. (2021). Unkept promises: State cuts to higher education threaten access and equity. Center on Budget and Policy Priorities.

Mullan, F., Chen, C., Petterson, S., Kolsky, G., & Spagnola, M. (2010). The social mission of medical education: Ranking the schools. Annals of Internal Medicine, 152(12), 804–811. https://doi.org/10.7326/0003-4819-152-12-201006150-00009

National Alliance on Mental Illness (NAMI). (2022). The economic cost of mental illness. Retrieved from https://www.nami.org

National Association of Realtors. (2022). Impact of student loan debt. https://www.nar.research

National Center for Education Statistics (NCES). (2022). Condition of education. U.S. Department of Education. Retrieved from https://nces.ed.gov

National College Health Assessment (NCHA). (2022). Impact of the COVID-19 pandemic on student mental health. Retrieved from https://www.acha.org

National Science Foundation. (2021). Survey of earned doctorates. Retrieved from https://www.nsf.gov

National Science Foundation. (2022). Growing convergence research. Retrieved from https://www.nsf.gov

Perna, L. W. (2018). Understanding the working college student: New research and its implications for policy and practice. Teachers College Record, 120(4), 1-15.

Posselt, J. R. (2016). Inside graduate admissions: Merit, diversity, and faculty gatekeeping. Harvard University Press.

Reardon, S. F., Kalogrides, D., & Shores, K. (2019). The geography of racial/ethnic test score gaps. American Journal of Sociology, 124(4), 1164–1221. https://doi.org/10.1086/701678

Reetz, D. R., Krylowicz, B., Mistler, B., & Bershad, C. (2021). The Association for University and College Counseling Center Directors Annual Survey. Journal of Counseling Psychology, 68(3), 315–330. https://doi.org/10.1037/cou0000478

Rogers, K. (2018). Financial mismanagement at the University of Akron: Prioritizing athletics over academics. Journal of Higher Education Policy and Management, 40(3), 230–245.

Rojstaczer, S., & Healy, C. (2012). Where A is ordinary: The evolution of American college grading. Teachers College Record, 114(7), 1–23.

Rudolph, F. (1990). The American college and university: A history. University of Georgia Press.

Sauermann, H., & Roach, M. (2012). Science PhD career preferences: Levels, changes, and advisor encouragement. PLoS ONE, 7(5), e36307.

Schulz, J. (2020). Funding disparities in STEM vs. humanities programs: A persistent challenge.

Simone, S. A. (2014). Transferability of postsecondary credit following student transfer or coenrollment. National Center for Education Statistics.

Soares, J. A. (2012). SAT wars: The case for test-optional admissions. Teachers College Press.

State Higher Education Executive Officers. (2020). State higher education finance: FY 2019.

Strada Education Network. (2022). The value of a college degree: Perceptions vs. realities. https://www.stradaeducation.org

Symonds, W. C., Schwartz, R. B., & Ferguson, R. (2011). Pathways to prosperity: Meeting the challenge of preparing young Americans for the 21st century. Harvard Graduate School of Education.

TICAS. (2021). Student debt and the class of 2021. Retrieved from https://ticas.org

The Institute for College Access and Success (TICAS). (2021). Student debt and the class of 2021. Retrieved from https://ticas.org

Thelin, J. R. (2011). A history of American higher education (2nd ed.). Johns Hopkins University Press.

Thelin, J. R. (2011). A history of American higher education (2nd ed.). Johns Hopkins University Press.

Twenge, J. M., & Campbell, W. K. (2018). Associations between screen time and lower psychological well-being among children and adolescents: Evidence from a population-based study. Computers in Human Behavior, 88, 47–54. https://doi.org/10.1016/j.chb.2018.06.029

USA Today. (2019). Clemson's $55M football complex sets new standard in college athletics. USA Today Sports.

U.S. Department of Education. (2023). Repayment of student loans: Average timelines. https://studentaid.gov

Vedder, R., Denhart, C., & Robe, J. (2013). Why are recent college graduates underemployed? University enrollments and labor-market realities. Center for College Affordability and Productivity.

Vedder, R. (2021). Restoring the promise: Higher education in America. Independent Institute.

Walsemann, K. M., Gee, G. C., & Gentile, D. (2015). Sick of our loans: Student borrowing and the mental health of young adults in the United States. Social Science & Medicine, 124, 85-93. https://doi.org/10.1016/j.socscimed.2014.11.027

Wilson, J. Q. (2019). The rise of political polarization in academia: Causes and consequences. Academic Inquiry, 15(3), 201–215. https://doi.org/10.1080/000913839234

Zimmerman, J. (2016). Campus politics: What everyone needs to know. Oxford University Press.

About the Author

Douglas B. Sims, PhD, is an accomplished environmental soil scientist with over three decades of experience, including more than 20 years in the environmental consulting industry, where he built and led successful companies across the nation. In 2011, he transitioned to higher education, bringing his extensive expertise to academia. Over the past 14 years, Dr. Sims has dedicated himself to advancing student success and workforce development, initially as an environmental science instructor and later as the Dean of the School of Science, Engineering, and Mathematics at a leading Nevada college.

Dr. Sims is widely published in peer-reviewed journals, contributing valuable research to his field. Beyond his professional accomplishments, he is deeply interested in human behavior, corporate dynamics, management, and leadership strategies. Married to his college sweetheart since the early 1990s, Dr. Sims and his wife have two grown children. Drawing on his unique blend of experience in industry and academia, Dr. Sims combines scientific expertise with a profound curiosity about leadership and organizational growth, offering a distinctive perspective that bridges both worlds.

www.ingramcontent.com/pod-product-compliance
Lightning Source LLC
Chambersburg PA
CBHW071726120626
46550CB00002B/400